17 Pieces

Dean Newby

Disclaimer

I have tried to recreate events, locales and conversations from my memories of them. In order to maintain their anonymity and protect their privacy in some instances I have changed the names of individuals and places.

Printed by Create Space

Copyright © 2013 Dean Newby

All rights reserved.

ISBN:1492195413
ISBN-13:9781492195412

For all who have loved, lost, and dared to love again

To my orsetto,
perhaps one day, I'll be writing a book about us and our life together!
Dae / 16/10/17

BONDED CIRCLE

When the pain of the world
Is screaming at you
And the tears of the children
Are drowning you

When the anger of stupidity
Is fighting against you
When the emptiness of loneliness
Is smothering you

I will reach for you
And hand in hand
We will form a bonded circle

And as the darkness encompassed you
We shall encompass the darkness
And as we tighten our circular grip
We will flood it with our light

Darkness will dissolve
Light shall reign
It does so because of how we are

We are responsible for it

Dean Newby, December 2004

CONTENTS

Preface

Acknowledgements

Introduction

1	Dear Zack (of Marble Arch)	1
2	Summer Something	7
3	The Italian Stallion	15
4	Unrequited U	21
5	Hair Today	49
6	The Mothers	59
7	One Eye On The Ground	83
8	In Safe Hands	95
9	Love…?!	103

10	I'm Coming Out…	111
11	The Girls Are Back In Town	119
12	Equals With A Side Of Pork	139
13	Lost Love, Lost Us	147
14	Chain Reaction	153
15	Defenders Of The Faith	163
16	Music Seen	169
17	London Found	181
	Afterword	203
	The Kickstarter Project	211
	References	216
	About the Author	218

PREFACE

The idea for 17 Pieces came from a friend's reaction to a bad-sad situation. I had recently broken up with a man I adored, Zack (of Marble Arch, and Piece 1), and by adored, I mean I had the Romeo & Juliet, travel to the ends of the earth kind of love for him.

A few days after telling my friend George about the demise of my relationship, as I was trudging to work, still angry at the world and my broken heart, shouting in my head, I received a text message from him, which simply read:

"I'm sorry your heart has been broken into 17 Pieces. I'll try and get them back for you"

followed a few days later by:

"I've found 1 piece, it was in a drawer next to his bed! 16 more to go!"

His messages were meant purely to lift my spirits, which they did! But, they also conjured an image in my mind, something that would soon become the idea behind this book.

The imagined image was of a glass heart falling to the floor and shattering into 17 pieces. On each piece was engraved a name, and a story to tell. I imagined myself collecting those pieces, those stories, and through telling their stories, being able to reassemble and mend that shattered, broken heart. Those stories, the writing and sharing of them, were the only way that the heart, my heart, could be truly healed, and made whole again.

Dean Newby

This book is about those 17 Pieces, pieces of a story from a life of loving, of the multitudinous forms that love can take; the love of a friend, a mentor, a place, the love felt from people's reactions to life altering news, and, of course, romantic love - known and unknown.

Those text messages were received, and the 17 shattered pieces of that glass heart were strewn across the floor of my mind two and a half years ago. This book has been written over about two years of that period, each piece written and re-written independently of the others, each one as a standalone piece, a story in its own right, but that when gathered together, assembled, reveal a story of a life of loving.

It is no surprise to me, or indeed to anyone involved in the writing of this book, that the subject matter of it, the first book I feel confident enough to publish, that I want to share with you, the reader, is love and the many forms it can take.

Why? Simply, because love is something that I have always been surrounded by, that I recognise in the eyes of strangers and the arms of friends. Love is something that I have experienced and been aware of for the entirety of my life, something that I have relished and revelled in, and something that I have, at times, lost. Love is something that I see and treat as a gift, probably the greatest gift we can give and receive. Love is the combination of all that is good about humanity, and still it has that unknown, indescribable factor, that characteristic whose indefinable nature is at the very core of, is the very essence of the true meaning of love.

This appreciation and recognition of love and its existence in many forms, is in part due to my being from a family whose closeness and respect for one another is, in my experience, unrivalled. Our love goes beyond the bond that is family, it is a love of the individual, not simply their familial position, with many of us treating each other as lifelong friends, rather than members of the same or similar genetic group. 'Family', to me, is not defined by genetics, it is defined by the love, care, respect, and support we show for one another.

On the lighter, less philosophical side, my ideas of what love is, are also in part due to the fact that I am the product of 80's pop and 90's divas (thanks to Ma Newby), the romanticism and rhythm of Motown (thanks to my grandad), the tradition of Irish Folksong and the storytelling and hope of Bob Dylan (thanks to my nan, Binkie), and I was the child who watched as Errol Flynn's Robin Hood fought the evil John and his followers, utterly beside myself with excitement and hope, anticipation and belief in Robin's cause, as hidden identities were revealed and sword fights were shown in shadow.

I am the product of early morning discussions, watching as dawn broke in the distance. I am the product of stargazing in the back garden, of wondering, pondering what lies beyond us and our planet. I am the product of bonfire nights with my cousins, sitting on old sofas in the garden as we ate soup, sausages, and stuffed cheesy potatoes.

I am the product of all of this, and so much more.
This book is the product of all of this, and all of me.

Dean Newby, London, 17th August 2013

Dean Newby

ACKNOWLEDGEMENTS

There are several (hundred) people I would like to acknowledge and thank for their part in the creation of this book, from those with whom I shared life experiences, some of which are contained herein, to those I discussed my initial ideas and thoughts for and about this book with. I think, indeed, I hope, that you all know who you are. If you think you might be one of these people, then you probably are.

However, there some people in particular that I want to single out and thank. These people are those who have played an integral part in either my life or in the writing of this book, I suppose, since the stories and writings contained in this book are the result of my experiences, and as such those I have shared said experiences with, it could be argued that the two groups are in fact one and the same, simply: those who have played an integral part

My Mum, Ma Newby, Maura Anne Newby (nee. Robinson) whose unwavering support of my hopes and dreams has been the lifeforce and fuel of my writing and so many other things I've done and achieved in my life. She gave me the tools, time and self-belief needed to write and explore my dreams, she is the person whose hand I know is always firmly on my back, supporting me, pushing me forward, encouraging me to set my sights on the seemingly unobtainable, on my true potential. Always secure in the knowledge that should I fall, she will be there to catch me, bandage my wounds, and put me back on my path. She is always a perfect balance of idealism and realism.

Dean Newby

My good friends:

Tom, whose care and support knows no bounds, whose honesty, directness and realism is balanced by his good heart and idealism. He has always been there for me, regardless of how busy he is, always with an encouraging word or piece of advice. Few people make me think as much as he does. Few people make me believe in myself as much as he does.

Rich, with whom I can talk about absolutely anything, aware that his reply will never be judgement-laden, that any advice he gives comes from a place of friendship, respect and care. One of the first people I spoke to about this book, one of the first people who told me to go for it, to at least try. The person off whom I bounced several ideas, sometimes at lightning fast, stream of consciousness speed, Rich always keeping up, listening, considering, ready to give his thoughts and ideas.

Danni, for always being able to break a bad or sad mood, for showing me what I have to offer, and for making me believe in love again, at a time when I thought I'd had my one and only chance.

Brooke, for her constant enthusiasm and encouragement about this book and everything else in my and our lives. For her constant questions and requests for updates about this book and its writing, for her suggestions and reminders about events and stories past, some of which have been included. For inspiring me to keep writing, to keep loving.
Last but by no means least, my *Kickstarter Pledgers & Backers*, those who pledged their hard earned money to ensure that this book could and would be published, most of them friends and family, some of them entirely unknown to me.

17 Pieces

Without them, the pieces of this book would still be sitting gathering digital-dust on my computer's hard disk drive.

Of the Kickstarter Pledgers, there are 8 who pledged at the 'Piece Signs' level and as such, their names can be seen below, on the:

Honour Role of Piece Printers

Ben Cooper

Bridget Taylor

Ed Robinson

Mauranne Newby

Sean O'Hagan

Sharon Kalsi

Tom Burke

The names of all 17 Pieces Kickstarter Pledgers (17 Pieces Believers) can be seen here: www.17pieces.co.uk/believers

Without all of these people, this book simply would not exist.

Thank you.

Dean Newby

INTRODUCTION

In short, 17 Pieces is about love. Love between man & man, man & woman, between friends, between relatives, love of things, and love of those who do not love us back. It is also about my love of love, of having respect for it, of nurturing it, of ensuring that my life is lived in as loving a way as possible - despite the many difficulties and challenges of such a goal.

Love is a universal thing. It is something we all feel in some way throughout our lives, it is something that should be celebrated, especially in an age when the downfall of celebrities seems to be the opiate of the masses, when all around us every day we hear and see sadness and anger, fear and resentment. Love is the one thing that can defeat those things, that can give us the strength to stand up and fight, to stand up and say what needs to be said, to stand up and help not only ourselves, friends and family, but also strangers who cross our life's path.

I am not arrogant or presumptuous enough to believe that my book, this book, will fill you with the same fighting spirit and enthusiasm that I have when it comes to love and the defence of that love. But, I do, and this is inextricably linked to my sense of just how important love is, hope that it can, even more, that it will.

As a reader, there have been books that I have read that have filled me with hope, have inspired me to do something, to aim higher, to be someone, just as there are books that have left me so incensed that I have had no other choice but to act.

Dean Newby

Words can be one of the most powerful forces of nature.

The words, stories and writings - collectively, the pieces, in this book are all of an autobiographical nature. Though some of them are semi-fictional, that fiction is based on a feeling or imagining I once had, influenced by previous experiences and feelings, and based on, at least in part, a memory.

The pieces are not in any sort of chronological order, rather they are in four loosely-based groupings of: 'Boys, Boys, Boys' (1-5), 'Family' (6-10), 'Friends? Forever?' (11-14), and 'Speak, Hear, Do' (15-17)

The first of the pieces is a letter to Zack, a letter which I had started writing long before I had thought about writing and publishing 17 Pieces. It was one of those letters you never send, that TV therapists of the 90's encouraged everyone to write. I subscribe to the idea of Unsent Letters, the catharsis of that simple act is one of the most healing things I have ever experienced. Once written, you can let it go, you can get over it.

The letter to Zack is one of five 'Core Pieces', pieces without which this book just wouldn't be the same. The remaining four pieces are:

> Summer Something
> a story of love and friendship
>
> One eye on the ground
> a story of life lessons from my grandad

17 Pieces

The Mothers
stories of my love of strong women and the principles they have taught me

I'm coming out...
the story of what happened when I came out to my family and friends

The value or importance of the remaining 12 pieces, though not part of the Core Five, should not be underestimated. In these pieces, several themes are covered, from that of unrequited love, in 'Unrequited U' (Piece 4), where you, the reader, are presented with the challenge of choosing which actions to take at various junctures in a relationship, to 'The Italian Stallion' (Piece 3) where you will read about a teenage crush and the start of something bigger...my love of Italian men.

In two of the semi-fictional pieces - 5 and 9, you will read about a man who has a minor breakdown on the London Underground, and the reliving of memories between a grandad and his grandson. Piece 8, 'In Safe Hands' is a set of memories of the love of a family member, while 'The Girls are back in Town' (Piece 11) is the story of how I met some of my female friends, accompanied by some of the single snapshot memories I've made with them, from the days of High School to the present. 'Equals with a side of Pork' (Piece 12) deals with a one-of-a-kind early-in-life friendship, while Piece 13, 'Lost Love, Lost Us' deals with the potential loss of a friendship, and Piece 14, 'Chain Reaction' with the actual loss of a friendship and the events that played a part in that loss.

Dean Newby

Piece 15, 'Defenders of the Faith' deals with my love, admiration and respect for those who stand up for what they know to be right, even in the face of absolute adversity. Piece 16, 'Music Seen' explains my love of music and what I feel and see when I hear certain songs, while the last piece, Piece 17, 'London Found' deals with my late-in-life love of London and some of its wonderful places.

Some of the pieces are written in a different style or format to the others, such as the Interview in 'Equals with a side of Pork', the letters of 'Dear Zack (of Marble Arch)' and 'Lost Love, Lost Us', the script-like nature of 'The Italian Stallion', and the Choose Your Own Adventure that is 'Unrequited U'. These styles and formats were chosen as they seemed to be the best way to communicate the stories, ideas and themes of those pieces to you, the reader. I think they do, indeed I now can't imagine them written in any other way.

Each piece was written independently of the others, and as such some details may be repeated between pieces, these details, however, are relevant to the pieces they are in, and as such have not been edited out.

17 Pieces

BOYS, BOYS, BOYS

PIECES 1 - 5

Dean Newby

1 / 17
DEAR ZACK (OF MARBLE ARCH)

Dear Zack,

I hope this finds you well, I really, sincerely do.

Of course, if we still saw each other, I'd know how you were, not just from your words, but from your beautiful and always too open eyes, they always did betray you.

Still, I doubt we'll see each other again, perhaps it's too difficult for both of us, or more likely just me, just as it may indeed be too 'difficult' for the then former and now very much present other half.

On that, I wanted to tell you something. This, by the way, requires no reply. Indeed, my self-respect and instinct for self-preservation do not allow me to seek a reply, only to tell you how I felt and feel, thought and think. Simply, I hope he makes you happy. I hope you build a life together that is all you want it to be. You deserve that, both of you do.

Dean Newby

It's taken me over a year to be able to say that, sincerely, for no reason other than probably the simplest of them of all; the love I felt for you, for us - the love that you took, enjoyed, and then destroyed.

I've never loved, nor do I think will ever love anyone the same way again. You touched my heart and my soul in a way it had never been, every touch felt alive, you made me feel like we were dancing our arses off to the best songs, our songs, over and over again.

That sense of possibility, of any and all options being open to me, all at a time when I was losing hope in the world, when so many questions seemed unanswerable. Your love, however short lived, enabled me to find myself, to hold myself upright, confident in the knowledge that should I falter you'd be there to hold me, to steady my footing as I walk the unknown line of life.

Well, you're not here anymore, neither in love nor in friendship.

That's ok, now. You went back to the man you love, and as much as my heart may have hurt because of that, I can't be angry about it. Being angry about love just doesn't fit with me.

Nor can I really be angry, anymore, about any mistreatment that may have befallen me - and, though you may deny it or do not want to hear of it, it did exist, I experienced it! But, in our time on this planet, we all do things that hurt others, no matter how hard we try not to, or how good our intentions are.

That is probably humanity's greatest flaw.

There are, however, a few things I want to share with you. Memories of us both in friendship and love. Some happy, some not, just like life - a collection of the ups and the downs, the times we laugh and the times we cry. I remind myself of the good times, including ours, when the world seems most against me, and try to forget the bad, though, no story, especially the one of life, is really all good, is it?

All the times we chatted about things you and I had in common with each other and no one else. Finally someone I could geek out with, talk tech news with, and who loved little-heard-of musicians and songs the same way I did. That, and a love of red wine and too much cheese was probably the founding of our friendship.

Remember the night we first realised that something was going to happen between us? When we both looked at each other, and smiled warmly, knowingly. Those smiles are so rare.

That night we got back to yours from the club. The night your flatmate thought we were drunk (we were) and 'crashing about'. Do you remember that? I still regret that I wasn't there when she asked you about that. I've no doubt your face would have been a picture.

That afternoon at yours, when we were going to watch DVDs and pig out on pizza and beer. Your flatmate, still not knowing (she must have known!) that there was anything going on between us. She was in the living room, you and I were chatting in the kitchen while you cooked. No, the memory isn't simply that you were cooking - though that was a unique experience in itself!

Dean Newby

You turned and kissed me. Delicately. Warmly. Up to that point we'd been all about the passion.

Of course, that night that we bumped into a mutual friend and you panicked, not knowing what he'd say or think. Not comfortable until he'd gone. As if he might go back and tell your ex that he'd seen two friends out together, perish the thought! Perhaps I should have known or at least suspected then that this was not going to go the way I wanted.

Then there's the night that you ripped my heart from my chest with blunted words, but even while doing so, you embraced me, your eyes welling up as you spoke. That spoke to me, and though my heart was being torn apart, the fact that you obviously cared, helped - a little at least. It made me feel secure in our friendship, despite this 'us' ending. But, I was wrong wasn't I? You're not here anymore.

I still remember, for I am as you know, cursed with a memory of people, you posing a hypothetical question of one of us getting a boyfriend, I immediately thinking to myself that we could be each other's. I, in my usual, as George would say, unashamedly direct way, calling you on it, stating not asking, that you were talking about getting back with your ex. From then, you tried to explain, and I have to give it to you, it was a valiant and seemingly sincere effort on your part.

That was probably the first time in my life that I have no recollection of when my tears started. I went from dry cheeks to an entire face covered in tears. Crying silently. Wanting so much not to let you go, not to allow this to happen. But, of course, I had no control over it. Whatever you felt for me, and I for you, just wasn't enough.

17 Pieces

I think one of the hardest things has been coming to terms with my heart being right for a time, then so horribly wrong and misguided. If I can't trust my heart, or as others would call it, my gut, what can I trust?! Well, I realised that my gut impression of you has never changed, the core of your being is good, you just can't and don't deal with things well or properly, or at least you don't the majority of the time.

You hurt me.

Despite how much you may not have wanted to, you hurt me when you broke my heart. But, that I can accept. Now.

The deeper hurt was the undiscussed, sudden dissolving of our friendship on your part. I had no role in that, that was all you, and it was totally undeserved. I had been an outstanding friend to you as I am to all those I consider good friends. I have come to accept what you did now, but I shall never understand it. I would not have been able to do that to you, not then, not ever. I couldn't.

You had me once, and you could have had me forever. All of me. All of my heart would have been yours for eternity. Instead, you took that heart and smashed it into 17 pieces, scattering them into the darkness and coldness of the winter's night.

Collecting those pieces and reassembling them has been an absolute bitch.

But, with a lot of time, patience, self-reflection, and thanks largely to my wonderful and ever-present friends, I did just that. An incredible thing happened upon the reassembly of my pieces, I realised that for the cracks to truly heal and vanish, for my heart to become truly whole again, I had to write this letter, and end it with a very simple message.

Goodbye Zack.

2 / 17
SUMMER SOMETHING

In the spring of 2008, I met a man named Isaac.

I was in Soho with LGBT Labour, leafleting and talking to voters, trying to persuade them to vote for Ken Livingstone in the upcoming London Elections. After the campaigning session, we all headed to a nearby bar for a much deserved drink and rest. I bought a Jack and Coke and joined our then Secretary who was standing near a small group of fellow campaigners.

He introduced me to the group, and after a while suggested that there was someone else I should also meet - I don't know why this person stuck out in his mind, considering that he and I had only just met too, but he did. He took me over to where 3 or 4 others were sitting, and looking beyond them, he introduced me. "Isaac, this is Dean. Dean, Isaac. Chat" and then he sauntered off to another group.

Isaac shuffled over in his seat, and I sat down next to him.

Dean Newby

We did as instructed, we chatted.

We had a few drinks, lots of laughs, and a whole lot of conversation. In fact, the conversation never ceased.

He was cute, funny, clearly intelligent and had a flair for bitch-wit.

Little did I know then, that he would soon come to play a huge part in my life. I wasn't even looking for anything at the time, but I guess that's when they say it happens, don't they?

After that first meeting, we chatted online every now and then, we met up for dinners and drinks, and eventually we started chatting, in some form or another, every day. All the while it becoming more and more apparent to me that this was the man I wanted. That first spark had grown into a blaze, and I didn't want anyone or anything to put it out.

One evening, having spent about an hour chatting online, he sent a message which still to this day makes me laugh:

"Are you ever going to ask me out?!"

This, by the way, is very him! To submissively initiate, laying the breadcrumbs, lighting the way, but making you, or me at least, take the lead.

He is worth the effort.

With my reply of "Yes", came one of his catchphrases:

"Well, jog on!"

So, I did just that, I asked him out, he played the comedian with lots of "Erms..." and "Let me check my diary...nope, not free until next July" before saying "Yes, of course, where? When? What's the plan? You do have a plan don't you?" - this is all, just to clarify, said entirely for comedic effect on his part.

And so began our 'relationship' - he'll appreciate the ".

Things started off well. Well, kind of well.

We had our first date, seeing a friend's photography exhibition at an East London warehouse gallery, followed by dinner - during which he spent an inordinate amount of time on his phone, and this was in the days before Grindr, so who knows what he could have been doing! But, things greatly improved by the second date, and soon we were having regular dates, great dates, nothing complicated or showy, just very us dates, down to earth, dinners, drinks and the cinema, DVDs and dinner at mine - after which he once came into the kitchen, and we just stood there cuddling, his arms around me. Those are the moments.

We went to various Prides with LGBT Labour, and spent the summer drinking and relaxing in the sun and in each other's company, we hadn't labelled it yet, but it was a summer something, and I was loving it. He'd spend the night at mine, then I'd walk him to the tube station for his commute to work, buy a newspaper and head home to watch the 'Gilmore Girls' and plan the rest of my day - it was August and all of my clients were closed for the Summer Holidays. He once had to borrow one of my ties for a meeting, I'm sure he still has it!

Dean Newby

Two months into it, and along came my birthday - the first and only birthday where I have been dating someone. He asked what I wanted to do, I chose the cinema, 'The Strangers' being my choice of film, because, you know, it's always wise to go to a film in which masks play a prominent part, when masks or hidden faces are your biggest fear!

When he arrived at the cinema, he gave me a potted sunflower (my favourite flower), still to this day, one of the best presents I've ever received, as well as a book about Ken Livingstone and a DVD of 'The Simpsons' Movie - he'd earlier been outraged by my having not seen it. We watched the film, my hands firmly gripping his arm the entire time, I'm surprised he wasn't bruised, but he sat there and took it. We got back to mine, I went and brushed my teeth and got ready for bed, but when I came back to my bedroom, the lights were off, and he wasn't there.

I heard a noise behind me, and as I turned, I saw, sat in my desk chair, a figure, face covered in some sort of white material, looking at me, breathing heavily. I screamed, punched, and then started laughing, probably fairly hysterically, only calming into a typical laugh when he took what was his white t-shirt off his face and revealed his stupidly cute smile, laughing the hardest I'd ever seen it. He still likes to remind me of that, and some of the terrifying words from the film, and bizarrely that is one of my favourite memories of our summer something.

As wonderful as this 'us' was, I knew that we had different ideas about what we wanted from each other, from this still fairly new 'relationship'. I wanted more than he was or at least at the beginning, had been willing to or could give - I should point out here, for the sake of fairness, that I knew from the start that he wasn't particularly interested in a relationship with me or anyone at that point in his life. But,

I was very much into him, and hoped that time and experience of what I had to offer would be enough to change his mind and/or heart, at that point I wasn't sure which ruled his life.

Even though, and perhaps because I could feel him gradually pulling away from me, from the us I wanted to be, I still needed to tell him how I felt and where I wanted us to go. It was time for the 'Exclusivity Chat'. We'd arranged to meet for coffee at St Pancras, one of our regular meeting places. As I arrived, my pulse quickening, nerves beginning to creep deep into the pit of my stomach, I thought about the last couple of months, how I'd felt, the things I'd done, and this person who had come into my life from out of nowhere and had made this enormous impact on me.

We got a coffee and found a seat. After some chit-chat, the standard "How has your day been?", that sort of thing, I was ready to say what I needed to. As I opened my mouth to speak, Isaac looked at me and said:

"Can I say something?"

Now, everyone knows the feeling you get when the person you're seeing says something like "We need to talk", it's that moment when you suddenly feel as if you're looking at yourself from the other side of the room, your mind blank with fear and panic because we all somehow instinctively know what that four word sentence means. I had that very same experience and feeling when Isaac asked his four word question.

He explained how he felt; that he really liked me but didn't see it, us, going anywhere. That I knew how he felt about relationships (which I did), that he didn't think it fair for us to continue seeing each other when he felt that way and I obviously felt another. Everything he said was fair, everything he said was true.

I sat silent for a moment, looking out of the plate glass window to the street ahead, watching as commuters went about their evening, buying dinner, reading the paper, unaware of what had just happened to me, to us. I wanted so much to run out of the doors and down that street into the evening's growing darkness. But, I also wanted to stay, to keep hold of the last few minutes we had together, the last few minutes of us.

I turned to face him, barely able to hold back my tears, and he once again started a conversation, something I will be forever grateful to him for because I'm not sure I could have spoken without crying. He said that he wanted to be friends, and I must have responded in some non-committal tone because he then looked me straight in the eyes and said:

"No, Dean, seriously, we are going to stay friends! Not like others say they will, we will!"

There was a sincerity to his voice and something about the way he was looking at me that made me believe him. I agreed, in an equally sincere and determined manner, got up and hugged him and the us that was, goodbye.

I got on the train, and as I sat staring out of the window, started to cry, so I picked up a newspaper to hide my face, not wanting anyone to ask what was wrong, and pretended to read. Not long into my tears, a Jamaican woman, dressed in a nurses uniform, sat next to me. I felt her glance at my face, then having reached deep into her handbag she pulled out a tissue and handed it to me, without saying a word. I took it, looked at her and thanked her. She smiled a warm, caring smile, the sort of smile only someone who has had their own share of sadness can smile, then said in a fantastically broad but soft Jamaican accent while patting my arm:

"Whatever it is, whoever it is. It'll all be al'righ'"

When I got home, I leaned against the hall wall, trying to regain some energy, some sort of strength, instead finding myself sliding down it, like a scene from some Hollywood tearjerker, my tears were heavier now than they had been, and my entire being was absolutely exhausted. I eventually managed to summon the strength to get up and put myself to bed, turning my phone off as I did, just wanting to be alone, away from the world.

A few days later, he left for America, volunteering for Barack Obama's first Presidential election campaign, and I went to Labour Party Conference in Manchester, seeing friends and fellow campaigners, discussing issues of education, health and internal politics, and most nights, getting very drunk and dancing my way from reception to reception.

But, Conferences are their own book of stories, one that can never be written, for what happens at Conference, stays at Conference!

Time passed, and I began to heal, helped both by his absence and the occasional message from him - he was making a real effort to pursue and secure the friendship we had both agreed to be a part of, and it was working.

Dean Newby

Soon, he returned from America, victorious, and our friendship continued on the same course it had been on before our foray into 'seeing each other', though, and I think he would agree, it was warmer, closer now.

Once you have loved, trusted, been entirely yourself with someone in the way that I was with Isaac, it can be all too easy to want to run, to hide yourself away from that person because they know too much, they've been privy to that which so few have been, and to see it in their eyes can be too much to bear.

But, if you can get over that, if you give yourself some time to get used to it, you can have something really quite special because of those things, after all there was a reason you were once attracted to each other, and I'm willing to bet it probably wasn't because of how hot or intelligent they were, or any of those other things we so often talk about when we talk about attraction. It is one of those indefinable things, a feeling, usually something about the way we feel about ourselves when we are with them.

Five years on and he is one of my closest friends and has been since his return. We see each other regularly, we talk about everything from work to men, friends to family, nothing is off limits, and both of us seek the other's thoughts and advice, all without any drama, any real effort, just he and I, talking, laughing, friends.

There are very few people I trust in this world as much as I do Isaac. That's a pretty special thing.

3 / 17
THE ITALIAN STALLION

<u>SCENE EXT. The Street</u>

Friends, Paul and Natalia are walking to Natalia's house after school. It is Spring.

Paul: I still don't understand why you let him treat you like that!? You must realise you can do better?!

Natalia: You don't understand, he isn't always like that. When we're alone together, he is lovely.

Paul: ...sometimes...

Natalia: Yes, sometimes! No one can be perfect every second of every day!

Paul: Except me. Obviously.

Paul takes a sideways glance at Natalia. She is trying to hide a smile.

Dean Newby

Paul: ...and you, of course!

Natalia: About time...that took you far too long! Anyway, I have spoken to him about it and he says he'll work on it.

Paul: He wants too!

Natalia *(laughing)*: ...or you'll sort him out?!

Paul: Natalia, you're Italian! There are any number of men from your family who would have a word with him!

Natalia: Can you imagine? I'd be grounded for all eternity, he'd be in the ground, and who would you walk home with?

Paul: I'd find someone, I'm sure. And I'd still pop around to see you...your family love me!

Natalia: Hmm. That is true, I don't get why!

Paul: Oh. Thanks.

Paul pretends to cross the road to escape Natalia. Natalia grabs him and links his arm.

Natalia: No, you know what I mean. You're the only friend my Dad talks to and asks about, and Ma is always inviting you around for dinner!

Paul: ...to fatten me up. *(Paul puffs out his cheeks and slouches)*

Natalia: Ha! She's Italian, she can't help it! She's a feeder, it seems to be her main goal in life!

Paul: ...and to find you a nice Italian boy to marry. Don't forget that!

Natalia: It's not as if she's trying to arrange a marriage or anything, besides Giovanni scares them all off!

Paul: The Italian boys? Or, just all boys?

Natalia: No, just the others, you know, the ones I'm actually interested in.

Paul: Like Charlie.

Natalia: Well done, you're far too good at bringing it back to what you want to talk about

Paul: What can I say? I'm skilled.

SCENE INT. Natalia's House, Hallway

As Paul & Natalia enter, they hear an upstairs door slam shut

Paul: Gio's obviously having a wank

Natalia: Urgh, vile! I don't want to think about that!

Paul: It's perfectly natural, I bet Charlie wanks all the time!

Natalia: Stop it! He doesn't actually, he says it's not the same.

Paul: HA! Yeah right! No offence. *(He winks)*

Natalia: Do you want a sandwich? Turkey-ham?

Paul: And you say your Ma is trying to fatten me up?!

Paul: *(pauses)* Yeah, that'd be good. I'm just gonna go to the toilet.

Natalia: *(shouts after him)* Don't go interrupting Gio!!

SCENE INT. Natalia's House, Upstairs

Paul knocks on Gio's door

Giovanni: Go away Nat, I'm busy!

Paul: Busy having a wank, eh Gio?

Giovanni: Oh it's you, hold on a minute...come in

Paul enters. Giovanni is on his bed in his boxers with a considerably noticeable bulge

Giovanni: Alright, stop staring! What's up?

Paul: Other than...*(Paul points at Giovanni's crotch and raises an eyebrow)*

Giovanni: Ha, cheeky git. Where's Natalia?

Paul: Downstairs

Giovanni: Making a sandwich?

Paul: How'd you guess?

Giovanni: *(shouts down to Natalia)* Nat make me one too, please!

Natalia: *(shouts)* Make one yourself! Paul, leave my brother alone!

Paul: *(shouts)* I wasn't doing anything. Promise!

SCENE INT. Natalia's Kitchen

Paul & Giovanni are hitting eachother as they walk into the kitchen - Giovanni is now wearing jogging bottoms

Natalia: Urgh, you two! Paul, here's yours, I put some crisps on the side too.

Paul: Aww, ain't you a love, you know me so well! *(Paul kisses her on the cheek)*

Giovanni: And, where's...*(Natalia hands him a plate with a sandwich on it)*

Giovanni: Oi, where are my crisps? Why does he get crisps and I don't?

Natalia: They're in the cupboard, get them yourself!

Giovanni takes a crisp off Paul's plate, licks it and puts it back. Paul takes the crisp and eats it.

Giovanni: Eww, you're so wrong! How could you eat that?

Paul: What? It's not as if you've got anything! Your mouth doesn't go anywhere!

Giovanni: Fair point.

Paul *(in a hushed voice)*: Except for when you're kissing some Italian Stallion

Giovanni: What did you say?

Paul: Me? Hmm? Nothing? Nothing Gio...

Natalia: Gio, go in the front room and be quiet!

Giovanni: Nat, I'm 18, 2 years older than you, you idiot!

Natalia goes upstairs to change, Giovanni goes into the front room, Paul to the conservatory.

Paul: Gio put some music on!

Paul hears a knocking on the glass door that separates the back room and the conservatory, he turns.

Giovanni is standing in front of the glass, holding the waistband of his jogging bottoms and boxers down, displaying his Italian schlong to Paul.

Paul looks, gives a nod of approval, followed by a wink.

Giovanni smiles broadly, pulls his waistband back up and goes back to eating his sandwich.

Paul turns, looks out at the garden and takes a bite of his sandwich.

Paul: *(thinking to himself)* And so it begins!

4 / 17
UNREQUITED U

Unrequited love can be an agonising, heartaching nightmare.

You find yourself standing staring at the object of your love, them having no clue that you are so totally and hopelessly into them, you not having the words (because no word or grouping of words is good or descriptive enough) let alone the courage to tell them how you feel; that you are so filled with love for them that you ache, you feel that you might explode if this goes on for much longer, that hopefully they feel the same way because a film told you that this is how life works...oh Hollywood, thou art a lying bitch sometimes.

I have had the misfortune of being the one whose love is unrequited, I like to think this is because I'm honest with myself about how I feel, and I am pretty black and white about most things, love being one such thing. The issue with that approach of course, is that for it to work, you

Dean Newby

need other people to think in a similar way. A lot of them don't.

There have been many (too many, really) occasions when my feelings for people have never been reciprocated. Or, if they are, they haven't been shared with me, not at least in any direct communication.

This is the story of one such occasion, the man involved, and what happened next...all in the style of a 'Choose your Own Adventure'

Starting at '1.' work your way through the piece, deciding what action you would take and then going to that action's corresponding number, and repeating the process until you come to the 'end'. On the last page of this piece, I've included a listing of the steps I took so that you can retrace them and see where you may have done something different to what I did.

Let the adventure begin...

17 Pieces

1.

You are out at post-campaigning drinks, when you meet a bloke called Ben.

Ben is funny, sweet, clearly intelligent and has one of those 'light up the room' smiles.

After some friendly new-person banter, your friends indicate that they want you to rejoin them.

Do you...

- ask for Ben's number (Go to: 15.)

- tell him it was nice to meet him, and rejoin your friends - you can ask your mutual friends about him later (Go to: 7.)

2.

Throughout the evening, you discuss everything from politics to art, men to hometowns, families to the future. Not once does the conversation dwindle or fall silent, not once do either of you lose interest in the other...despite the many pretty men walking by or standing at the bar, not once.

The bar calls last orders, and Ben looks at you...

Do you...

- suggest that it's home time (Go to: 41.)

- suggest "One more drink?" (Go to: 19.)

3.

Ben realises that he has perhaps not acted in the way a friend should, and so apologises, hugging you and suggesting that his friend isn't usually like that, it is just the drink talking. The rest of the group, except Ben's friend, join you and you all head to another friend's birthday party. When you get there, you meet a cute man who immediately starts chatting you up. You, aware that Ben is watching but has never once acted on the chemistry between you, and also liking what this new man has to say and offer, begin flirting back. He suggests that you leave the party and head back to his.

Do you...

- go and tell Ben that you are leaving and will give him a call tomorrow (Go to: 27.)

- tell the new man that you are out with friends and so have to decline his offer (Go to: 34.)

4.

A few weeks later, you and a friend are out at a political fundraiser, when Ben walks in.

Ben comes over and eagerly enters into conversation with you, asking about your weekend, what you like to do in your free time - Jeez, soon he'll want to know your favourite colour and the names of all of your cousins! You don't mind really, he's showing an interest...always a good thing!

A friend of yours comes over to where you and Ben are standing and begins flirting with Ben, obviously.

Do you...

- interject and start flirting with Ben yourself - hands off, you! (Go to: 23.)

- leave your friend to it (Go to: 11.)

5.

Upon hearing your suggestion that he is jealous, Ben reminds you that he took someone home last night. He then proceeds to tell you every single detail about him, including his 'Spanish chipolata'. He then puts his arm around you, and you begin to walk. Your soul is screaming from the image that has just been described to you.

Do you...

- put your arm around him, hiding your feelings about what he has just told you (Go to: 48.)

- tell him that you don't like it when he describes such things (Go to: 22.)

6.

A few months have now passed, and your friendship with Ben is continuing nicely, another few decades of this and you should finally have your man. You go to his apartment for a house party, getting there early to help setup. Throughout the night, Ben introduces you to a lot of new people, friends from University, old colleagues and new.

Dean Newby

They are all lovely, and all seem to have some prior knowledge of you. Ben is extremely attentive of you during the entirety of the evening, making sure you're having a good time, being very touchy-feely and huggy, even for him. It is too late to get a tube home, so you decide to spend the night on the sofa. As you lay there, drifting off, you hear a noise and feel a presence near you. You half open your eyes to see Ben standing in front of you in his boxer-briefs (quite the sight to see), clearly trying to determine whether you are awake or not.

Do you...

- open your eyes fully, aware of what will happen next (Go to: 45.)

- pretend to be asleep, if this is going to happen, it is going to happen when he is sober (Go to: 32.)

7.

Throughout the remainder of the evening, you notice Ben glancing over to where you're standing.

At one point, as you look up (you are after all also glancing in his direction), you catch him looking directly at you, you both smile, yours turns into a small laugh.

Do you...

- wink at Ben (Go to: 4.)

- walk over to Ben and ask him for his number (Go to: 15.)

8.

You return to Ben and his new friend, they are obviously attracted to each other. Ben introduces you as his friend. His friend. You make several attempts to block the cute man's advances, but it quickly becomes evident that you are going to fail. He and Ben soon leave the bar together.

(Go to: 29.)

9.

You, Ben and a group of friends enjoy a day trip out of London, seeing the sights of nearby villages. Upon returning to London, a drunken argument begins between a friend and an acquaintance (who is a good friend of Ben's). You intervene hoping to keep the peace and tranquility of the day intact. The acquaintance turns on you, calling you several names and acting like an utter tosser. Ben doesn't come to your defence.

Do you...

- implore him to do something (Go to: 55.)

- walk away from the table, you have better things to do with your time (Go to: 31.)

10.

Having told him to get over himself, Ben briefly laughs, then suggest that the two of you go clubbing together. Which you do. It's 10:30 the next morning, and after a night of some pretty hardcore dancing, you are fast asleep in bed,

Dean Newby

when your phone beeps. A text message from Ben. It asks if you want to go for breakfast and a wander around town.

Do you...

- jump at the chance (Go to: 17.)

- tell him that you are too hungover to operate, which you probably are (Go to: 36.)

11.

Ben sends you an e-mail, inviting you to an event he's organising.

You can't go, so you reply with a "thanks" and an apology for your scheduling conflict. Ben replies almost immediately and suggests that since you can't make that event, perhaps the two of you could go for a drink some other time.

Do you...

- accept Ben's invitation and arrange something there and then (Go to: 16.)

- accept Ben's invitation, but leave it open (Go to: 41.)

12.

You wait for the kiss for what seems like several minutes, but is, in fact, mere seconds. It never comes, and the moment passes into the darkness of the night. Your foreheads part company and you both begin walking again. Upon reaching the bar where your friends are, Ben goes and talks to one of his closest friends. You go to the bar where you are approached by the new man. He is not giving up.

Do you...

- cut your losses and go home with the new man (Go to: 28.)

- give the new man a definitive 'no, I'm not interested' and rejoin Ben and your friends (Go to: 6.)

13.

You get no response to your message.

It is time to move on, he clearly has.

Ben will always be the one who got away, there is no changing that now.

However I can and have learnt from that and now ensure I seize the opportunity to act on my feelings when it arises. Life is too short, and those opportunities too sparse.

Do you...

- agree: 'The End' (Go to: the next Piece, your work here is done)

- disagree (Go to: 1. start again, learn the lessons)

14.

Nothing happens at that point, except for another drink being drunk, and a lot of tipsy smiling and longing looks (from you). It's a week later, 23:30 on a Saturday night, and you've just got home from a day with the family, when your phone rings. You look at it and see Ben's name, so answer it. After a few minutes of chat and banter, Ben asks if you want to come over or go out somewhere.

Do you...

- make reference to the time and suggest this is a booty call (Go to: 26.)

- indicate that you'd like to go out dancing (Go to: 43.)

15.

Ben looks at you, why are you after his number when you have only just met?!

He suggests that instead you give him yours or your e-mail address, he'll be in touch.

Do you...

- insist he gives you his number (Go to: 30.)

- give him your number and e-mail address, you definitely want to hear from him (Go to: 11.)

16.

It is the evening of your drinks with Ben, you are nervous but looking forward to it.

You spend an inordinate amount of time choosing what to wear and 'styling' your hair, having already bathed for so long that your skin resembles the Grand Canyon's crevices. You get the bar purposefully early to get a drink, relax and arrange yourself accordingly.

When Ben arrives, do you:

- extend your hand to shake his (Go to: 35.)

- go in for a hug (Go to: 2.)

17.

You meet Ben at Bond Street, he hands you a coffee - exactly the way you like it. You do some shopping, he needs new underwear, giving you the chance to flirt some more. He mocks you for kissing that guy last night, he is right to mock, it was one of those drunken errors of judgement. But is that a hint of jealousy in his voice?

Do you...

- suggest that he is jealous (Go to: 5.)

- laugh it off (Go to: 40.)

18.

We are? Then male homosexuality is still illegal! You'd better hide this book, quickly. I was never here. Shh.

Climb into this time machine, and go back to your previous decision.

19.

You go for one more drink with Ben, which turns into two, then three. You notice that he is gradually moving closer to you, slowly but surely, you are not entirely sure what this means, but you like it.

Do you...

- move closer and put your arm around him in one smooth action (Go to: 14.)

- suggest it is time to go home (Go to: 41.)

20.

Boy did you give up easily! Are you sure you are really interested in this Ben?

- yes (Go to: 11.)

- hmm...maybe not (Go to: 38.)

17 Pieces

21.

The housemate seems annoyed by your half-joking half-serious defence and suggestion that he was trying it on. You and Ben laugh it off, it was an innocent mid-sleep cuddle, we've all been there. You leave the apartment and head home to your own bed, very much in need of more sleep. A couple of days pass, and you haven't heard anything from Ben. You send him a text message but get no response, so eventually send him an e-mail. Weeks pass and still there is no response from Ben. You go to a campaigning session and then the post-campaign drinks, where you see Ben.

Do you...

- go up to him and ask him why he hasn't replied to any of your messages (Go to: 50.)

- ignore him, you have made the effort, it is his turn. If he comes up to you, then you will make further effort (Go to: 33.)

22.

You and Ben start spending a lot more time together, sometimes whole weekends doing London things together, or watching films and reading newspapers over coffee by the Thames. There are times when the chemistry between you is on full throttle, and it feels as if you are more than friends - despite nothing physical having yet happened.

Do you...

- try to make something physical happen (Go to: 45.)

- start making subtle hints about how you feel about him (Go to: 9.)

23.

Your friend becomes frustrated by your obvious (to him at least) attempts to block and outdo his flirting with Ben. He starts having a go at you, claiming that you are not a good friend because friends don't do that to each other.

Do you...

- realise that your friend is right, so pull him to the side to explain that you have a thing for Ben (Go to: 37.)

- realise that your friend is right, so stop your flirting and allow him to get on with it (Go to 11.)

24.

A year passes, then two. You still find yourself thinking about Ben every now and then, usually because of revisiting one of the places where you used to spend time together, or because a programme he would love is on TV. You want to reconnect, but are unsure if you should, you do have self-respect after all.

Do you...

- send him a simple message asking how he is, what he is up to (Go to: 52.)

- send him a message telling him how much you miss him and that you hope you can one day rekindle whatever it was you once had (Go to: 13.)

25.

You meet up the next day, both hungover, both a little nervous.

Ben starts the conversation. "I was so drunk last night! Ha, I can't believe we kissed! Stupid drunkenness! That's what it was!"

Do you...

- disagree that it was simply 'Stupid drunkenness', deciding that it is time to tell him how you truly feel (Go to: 42.)

- agree, he clearly doesn't want anything more than friendship. Don't torture him or yourself any further (Go to: 6.)

26.

Upon suggesting that this late night call seems like a booty call, and subtly hinting that you might be up for that, Ben laughs then asks if you are flirting with him?

Do you...

Dean Newby

- laugh and tell him to get over himself (Go to: 10.)

- tell him that you are, it's about time he noticed (Go to: 39.)

27.

Upon hearing that you are leaving, Ben grabs you and asks you to stay with him at the party, he needs to know that everything between you is ok.

Do you...

- reassure him that everything is fine between you and leave with the new man (Go to: 28.)

- reassure him that everything is fine between you, but stay with him to prove it (Go to: 34.)

28.

You wake up in the new man's bed the next day, head aching and in need of sustenance. You and the new man go to a cafe down the road for breakfast, then a coffee, followed by a walk and then lunch. As you sit at the table, you receive a text message from Ben. It reads: "What time did you leave last night? I don't remember anything after the last drink at the party!" You know this is his way of saying "Lets not talk about what happened last night"

Do you...

- do as he implies and never mention the near-kiss of the previous night (Go to: 6.)

- ignore his message and arrange to meet up for a chat later that day (Go to: 46.)

29.

Go to the Friend Zone and spend an eternity there as 'just good friends'.

Return to your last decision. Think again.

30.

Well done, your persistence has sent Ben running for the hills! You've only just met after all!!

(Go to: 1.) and try again, maybe this time you'll get beyond your first meeting with him. Jeez.

31.

Ben follows you away from the table, and upon catching up to you asks why you are so upset. You begin to tell him that it is both the argument itself and the fact that he didn't defend you against his friend, your acquaintance, that has so upset you. He suggests that you shouldn't have got involved, and certainly shouldn't be dragging him into it.

Do you...

- tell him that he needs to be a better friend because you would never let that happen to him (Go to: 3.)

- tell him that you don't want to talk about it, and make your way to your friend's party (Go to: 54.)

32.

Ben, thinking you are asleep, leaves the room. You, realising that the sofa is actually quite uncomfortable, go into his housemate's bedroom and into the empty space in his bed - which had previously been offered to you anyway. During the night, you wake up to find the housemate cuddling you in his sleep. In the morning, you wake to find the housemate gone, and upon getting up you hear him telling Ben about your being in his bed. As you approach them, they both raise their eyebrows, and Ben suggests, in a seemingly joking tone, that you were "trying it on" with his housemate.

Do you...

- deny all charges and laugh it off (Go to: 49.)

- tell Ben that it was, in fact, his housemate who was doing the hugging, so... (Go to: 21.)

33.

You ignore him, and he doesn't come up to you. Instead, he stands talking to friends, not once looking in your direction. Your heart sinks entirely, what has happened? You haven't done anything wrong, there is no reason for this to be happening to your friendship with Ben. Soon he leaves the bar, not even coming to say goodbye to you.

Do you...

- send him a message asking what all that was about (Go to: 51)

- decide that it, whatever 'it' was, is over, he is gone (Go to: 24.)

34.

As the party draws to a close, you all leave to find another bar. You and Ben are both pretty drunk by now, and having waited behind to finish your drinks, are now several streets behind your friends. Ben puts his arm around your waist, and the two of you leave the bar. Ben stops in the street, and turning to face you, puts his arms around your back and draws you in for a hug. His lips and yours are an inch apart, foreheads resting against each other.

Do you...

- seize the opportunity and go in for a kiss (Go to: 47.)

- wait for him to kiss you (Go to: 12.)

35.

(from 16.) You shook his hand? Seriously, what is actually wrong with you? Are we in Victorian Britain?

- we are (Go to: 18.)

- no, we're not, I'm just a traditionalist (Go to: 44.)

36.

How do you ever expect to get Ben when you don't take the opportunity to spend 1:1 time with him? Huh?!

Man up, drag yourself out of bed, shower and (Go to: 17.) to spend some quality Sunday afternoon time with Ben!

37.

Your friend, having been told that you are interested in Ben, that he is the one you told him about, apologises to you and then proceeds to come up with a strategy to help you get Ben. As you discuss strategy, Ben is approached by a cute man who immediately strikes up conversation.

Do you...

- hurry back to Ben, you've just managed to stop your friend flirting, now there's this guy to deal with! (Go to: 8.)

- admit defeat for now, there will be other opportunities. Won't there?! (Go to: 20.)

38.

Do not pass through their bedroom door.

Return to your last decision. Think again.

17 Pieces

39.

Silence. You ask if he is ok. Still silent, Ben is never silent.

Finally, he speaks, telling you he likes you, but not in that way...he thought you realised you were just friends. He thinks you're cute, but you are just friends.

I get it, we're just friends. I'll be off to the Friend Zone then...while there perhaps you (dear reader) should go over your previous decisions to see how we got to this point?

40.

You laugh off your drunken error of judgement, we have all been there! You spend the rest of the day together, chatting about work, life, the usual. It is one of those lovely Sunday afternoons that make the following Monday a little more bearable.

(Go to: 22)

41.

After a couple of weeks of no contact from Ben...

Do you...

- send him an e-mail suggesting a drink in the next couple of weeks, perhaps this Friday? (Go to: 16.)

- assume that he isn't interested in pursuing a friendship (Go to: 20.)

Dean Newby

42.

Here is where the story ends.

At the time of my unrequited love for Ben, it is at this point that I would have hoped he would come running into my arms, telling me that he felt the same way as I did, and just used the drunkenness excuse because he didn't want to scare me off. We would then, of course, live happily ever after.

However, there is also the possibility that the opposite could have happened, and so: (Go to: 39.)

43.

You and Ben go out clubbing. After a night of some pretty hardcore dancing, you are fast asleep in bed, when your phone beeps. A text message from Ben. It asks if you want to go for breakfast and a wander around town.

Do you...

- jump at the chance (Go to: 17.)

- tell him that you are too hungover to operate, which you probably are (Go to: 36.)

44.

A traditionalist you say? Very well, but do you really see anything romantic happening from a handshake?

No, neither do I, and you could be confining yourself to the category of 'Friend' or worse, 'Acquaintance'.

17 Pieces

Perhaps you should go back to your previous decision and re-examine whether 'traditional' is the best approach to take.

45.

You wake up in Ben's bed. Both of you naked.

What were you thinking? Sure, it was awesome at the time, but now it's the morning after, the morning of awkward regret.

You cover your face with the duvet and will yourself back to the previous decision.

46.

You meet up later that day, both hungover. You are a little nervous.

You start the conversation. "Do you really not remember anything after the party? Do you not remember that we were a hair's breadth from kissing?"

Ben laughs and suggests that if that was the case, it was purely out of drunkenness and didn't mean anything.

Do you...

- disagree that it was simply 'Stupid drunkenness', deciding that it is time to tell him how you truly feel (Go to: 42.)

- agree, he clearly doesn't want anything more than friendship. Don't torture him or yourself any further (Go to: 6.)

47.

Wow! What a kiss. It's hardly surprising, he has such a great smile, and the chemistry has always been there. Even with drunken stumbling and swaying in the street, it was amazing. For so long you have wanted that kiss from him, and now you've had it! Huzzah!! Now, you both stand there in each other's arms, foreheads still pressed against each other. What's next?

Well, since this bit never happened, and is an entirely imagined fork in the road, it would seem there would be two options:

Do you...

- act as if nothing happened, there's the friendship to think about... (Go to: 6.)

- suggest that you need to talk about it, there's a lot to say, but when you are both sober... (Go to: 25.)

48.

Your ploy works, Ben didn't pick up on your feelings about his man from the previous night. Of course, by doing so, you have now opened the doors to his sharing everything about any future men...what were you thinking? You should have told him that you don't like him telling you everything, you can do that without telling him how you feel about him. For now, it seems as if looks like you're going to spend some time in the dungeon of the Friend Zone, tortured by descriptions of Ben's men.

17 Pieces

Quickly, escape the FZ using the 'Magical Potion of Decision Undoing' and go back to the last decision made.

49.

This attempt to laugh at the situation works for you and Ben, but his housemate doesn't seem amused. You leave the apartment and head home to your own bed, very much in need of more sleep. A couple of days pass, and you haven't heard anything from Ben. You send him a text message but get no response, so eventually send him an e-mail. Weeks pass and still there is no response from Ben. You go to a campaigning session and then the post-campaign drinks, where you see Ben.

Do you...

- go up to him and ask him why he hasn't replied to any of your messages (Go to: 50.)

- ignore him, you have made the effort, it is his turn. If he comes up to you, then you will make further effort (Go to: 33.)

50.

Ben ignores you, walking away from you and refusing to answer your question. What is going on?

Ben leaves the bar.

Do you...

Dean Newby

- follow him (Go to: 53.)

- decide that it, whatever 'it' was, is over, he is gone (Go to: 24.)

51.

Your message gets no response.

Do you...

- decide that it, whatever 'it' was, is over, he is gone (Go to: 24.)

- send him a message outlining your feelings for him (Go to: 42.)

52.

Your simple message gets no response.

You aren't particularly surprised, it has been a long time, it's rare to be able to pickup where you left off.

It is time to move on, he clearly has.

Ben will always be the one who got away, there is no changing that now.

However I can and have learnt from that and now ensure I seize the opportunity to act on my feelings when it arises. Life is too short, and those opportunities too sparse.

Do you...

- agree (Go to: the next Piece, your work here is done)

- disagree (Go to: 1. start again, learn the lessons)

53.

You follow him out of the bar, but still he ignores you, until finally you decide that you have to seize your opportunity, and in a moment of desperation, you blurt out how you feel about him. He stops walking.

(Go to: 42.)

54.

When you get to the party, you meet a cute man who immediately starts chatting you up. You, aware that Ben is watching but has never once acted on the chemistry between you, and also liking what this new man has to say and offer, begin flirting back. He suggests that you leave the party and head back to his.

Do you...

- go and tell Ben that you are leaving and will give him a call tomorrow (Go to: 27.)

- tell the new man that you are out with friends and so have to decline his offer (Go to: 34.)

55.

Ben looks at you and tells you that it isn't his place to intervene. So, you get up from the table and walk away from the group, you don't allow anyone to talk to you like that. Ben follows you away from the table, and upon catching up to you asks why you are so upset. You begin to tell him that it is both the argument itself and the fact that he didn't defend you against his friend, your acquaintance, that has so upset you. He suggests that you shouldn't have got involved, and certainly shouldn't be dragging him into it.

Do you...

- tell him that he needs to be a better friend because you would never let that happen to him (Go to: 3.)

- tell him that you don't want to talk about it, and make your way to your friend's party (Go to: 54.)

---End of the Choose Your Own Adventure Section---

So, how did you do? How long did it take you to reach 'the end'? How many moves?

There are shorter, easier ways to go about this sort of relationship and deal with the feelings it entails, but I, of course, took the longer, 27 step approach.

Here's what I did:

1, 7, 4, 11, 16, 2, 19, 14, 26,

10, 17, 5, 22, 9, 31, 3, 27, 34,

12, 28, 6, 32, 21, 33, 51, 24, 13.

5 / 17
HAIR TODAY

"The next station is Finchley Road." announced the bodiless voice of the London Underground.

Paul stepped off the train and walked across the platform to board the Southbound Metropolitan train that was waiting there, finding a seat near a window where he could rest his weary head.

It hadn't been an easy day; he'd woken up late, missed his bus, missed the start of the morning meeting, and all without even a sip of tea. So, by the time to leave came, he was exhausted and slumped deep into his chair. The slump had been the same since he and Zack had stopped seeing each other a few months ago, no matter what he did, he just couldn't get him out of his head, or worse still, his heart.

The tube departed the Overground and headed deep into the tunnel, the juddering carriage rocking Paul to a light sleep, all he did was nap these days, it had been a long time since he'd had a proper sleep, a peaceful sleep. He found nothing peaceful about feeling the cold hollow space beside him in his bed when he still reached across for a cuddle in the night.

As he entered that half-nap, half-aware state of a long time London transport user, his MP3 player played the soundtrack of his life, various 80's pop, some reggae, and more than a few ballads. He always felt safe with his soundtrack, it was a part of him, something that wouldn't change, something that would always stay the same, known, reliable.

As the train approached Great Portland Street, something, some noise or scent, something, made Paul open his eyes. With his head still leaning against the cold window, Paul's eyes focused, and directly in his line of sight, towards the other end of the carriage, and with back turned to him he saw what looked like Zack. He had the same bum, Paul would know that bum anywhere, he had the same shape - height and breadth, and he had the same hair, that hair. The hair he always played with when they kissed or were sat watching a film, such good hair.

Paul wasn't entirely sure how he had got from his seat to his current position, just a few inches away from Zack's back, but he was there now, rocking in time with the train, his frown deepening with every jolt. He became aware of the fact that the person in front of him may not actually be Zack, but it was too late, the fury was already rising to the surface, the taste of hot molten metal crept up his throat.

Paul opened his mouth to speak, his normally soft-gentle tone, replaced by a deep angry roar, a roar of anger and loneliness, sadness and emptiness:

17 Pieces

"Your hair! Change your hair! That's the hair only a heartless bastard would have!" he roared, fists clenched and shaking, eyes wide and fixed on the subject of his fury.

The poor boy, Paul's victim, turned and looked at his detractor with astonishment, confusion, indignation and a little fear. "What has just happened? I was talking to Charlotte, the train stopped, people got on, then...this. Shouting, no, shrieking! What did I do?"

"...what was that about my hair?!"

"And WHO are YOU?!"

When he'd finally stopped shouting, Paul stood there, suddenly aware of and stunned by his own behaviour. He only realised he was crying when he tasted his tears on his lips.

So many tears, but unlike his outburst, he was silent, not a whimper, not a whine, not even a sniff. Just him and his tears, alone. Always alone.

A girl, presumably Charlotte, looked at her friend to try and gather some sort of understanding of what had just happened, he looked back at her in stunned silence. He, like her, was clueless. But, she found "No one talks to my friends like that!" spitting from her mouth, and as she felt her body lurch forward, her friend moved his arms to stop her, that trusty barrier that had so often stopped her from doing something she would ultimately and usually immediately regret.

Peter knew all too well what would happen next were he to waiver in his suppression of Charlotte's natural protective instincts. There would be harsh words, aggression, potentially some sort of unnecessary physical contact. That was Charlotte, part of her anyway, and Peter could see that however upset and angered he and Charlotte were by this stranger's outburst, it was nothing compared to the stranger's anguish. What had happened to this man to make him act in such an irrational way? Something awful, surely.

And so, he stopped Charlotte, there was no other option. Charlotte was particularly unimpressed by this, but let it go, for now. She had always considered Peter to be the nice one, the kind one, the one who went out of his way to help other people, even people he didn't know. At first she had thought of this as a weakness, but now, several years into their friendship, she considered it one of the best characteristics anyone could ever have. She often told people at parties that the world needed more Peters, and it does.

Then, looking at the man, Peter took a tissue from his bag and handed it to him.

Paul crumpled to the floor in a mess of tears and regret, self-loathing and absolute anguish, his pain so strong and full that it had no sound, no words to say, and no voice to say them even if they had existed. He felt sick, he felt shaken, still shocked by his actions. So, when this man, this innocent victim of his egregious behaviour handed him a tissue for his tears, they came even quicker.

His unknown victim of his unprovoked attack pitied him enough to help him, when really he should have hit him, or at least let his scowling female friend hit him. She clearly wanted to, and from the look of her, she could have dealt quite some damage!

17 Pieces

Paul took the tissue and covered his eyes with it. If only he could just keep himself hidden until the train pulled into the next station, he could get off and find a place to hide, to recover, to work out what had just happened, if it had happened at all - this sort of thing doesn't just happen, not in real life, on TV perhaps, some dreadful reality TV show of nobodies and wannabes, but not him, not in real reality.

He sat for what seemed like a lifetime before removing the tissue from his eyes. As he opened them, he saw the man crouching beside him, and an elderly woman looking at him from her seat near the door, not with fear or disgust but with concern. Her eyes were sad but bright, grey with several flecks of her years splintering the sides of her face. She had lived, she had been through much, but still she was concerned for him. Why? Paul thought to himself, why is she, a perfect stranger, concerned for him? In that moment, in her expression, she had shown more concern for him and how he felt than anyone else had in quite some time.

Then, the woman leaned forward, took a roll of mints out of her purse and offered one to Paul. Still looking at her concerned, caring expression, He took one.

"You suck on dat now darlin'" she said in a broad Jamaican accent "Suck on dat and don't you worry"

Paul sat, eyes glazed and stinging from his tears. Everything, every part of his body, his being, hurt, when was everything going to stop hurting?!

As the train entered the next station, Paul could see Peter explaining something to Charlotte, her face stony cold, at least until, after a short pause, he said something very briefly to her, and she changed entirely. She gave him a smile, then a hug, and as she stepped out of the carriage, she looked to Paul and gave him a small, minuscule even, nod.

The door closed, and Peter sat himself down on the floor next to Paul. They sat quietly at first, until Paul cleared his throat to speak

"I'm sorry for all of that! I really am so truly sorry! I don't know you, we've never met, you must think I'm nuts!!"

Peter listened, then in a calming tone said

"I'm Peter. As for nuts...no. Hurting? God, yeah. But, we've all been there, and while you can't go around screaming at people, and you really, really can't...sometimes we just crack. It's temporary, and as long as temporary can seem sometimes, it is temporary"

Paul looked into Peter's eyes as he spoke, they weren't like Zack's, they were bright and happy, not the sleepy, come-to-bed eyes he'd loved for so long. There was a kindness in those eyes that he hadn't seen for far too long a time. He deserved to see, to experience that kind of kindness again.

Peter continued "I'm guessing, and it's a fairly educated guess from what I could make out during your screaming rampage, that your ex had similar hair to mine? Oh, and that he was a heartless bastard, of course"

Paul, who barely remembered, and was not sure he was entirely lucid during his outburst, though perhaps it was more a case of his trying to force his rampage out of his memory, was astonished by Peter's candidness. "Erm, yeah, his hair was exactly like yours, probably still is. I, I don't know, we don't see each other anymore." Paul said, aware that he owed Peter an explanation, and then some.

That seemed to make Peter's mind up for him. "Have you got anywhere you need to be? Fancy a coffee?"

Something in Peter's voice and his entire demeanour, the way he had transformed from victim to good samaritan, made Paul want to accept his offer of a coffee. So, he did.

As the pair departed the train and climbed the stairs, Peter started telling Paul about his recent ex...how he once saw him at a Tube Station. Peter was ascending the escalator and about halfway up he saw his ex, Greg at the top. Without thinking, he started trying to walk back down the escalator, bumping into people, tripping, causing problems for people simply trying to go about their Thursday evening. He inevitably failed, and so, having quickly straightened himself out, fixing his hair, wiping the sweat from his forehead, and plastering, what he was sure was a ridiculous smile across his face, he reached the top and walked over to Greg.

Of course, it wasn't Greg, it was just someone who looked a lot like him. Peter was relieved, and a little saddened, it would have been nice to see Greg again, they should have stayed friends post-breakup, but like so many others, they hadn't.

As Paul and Peter exited the station, Peter said something that would forever stay with Paul:

It's funny, isn't it, how we can see something that we don't think we want to, in something that may only share a passing resemblance, if any at all, to it. The mind needs what the heart wants.

Dean Newby

FAMILY

PIECES 6 - 10

Dean Newby

6 / 17
THE MOTHERS

I have been extremely fortunate to have some amazing people in my life, most of them women, whose strength, determination, passion, and sense of justice and fairness, I have, for many years, observed and learnt valuable lessons from. Those lessons, learnt from both direct teachings and observations of behaviour and personality, form a set of principles, beliefs and ways of behaving that are part of the core of my being.

They are the teachings of The Mothers.

I don't know why it is women who have usually taught me such things, perhaps it's something to do with my relationships with them to begin with, perhaps our relationships exist, at least in part, because they are the sort of people who have something to say, to teach, and so those characteristics are part of the basis of those relationships. Perhaps it is simply that I have a lot of strong, opinionated, and I hate that 'opinionated' is so often used in a derogatory fashion, women in my life, and I am open to hearing their opinions and beliefs? Whatever the reason, I am delighted that they have been there to teach, and I to learn.

I don't know the why, but I do know the who, the what and the when of some of the most important pieces of wisdom and principles they have imparted, sometimes without them even realising - that so often seems to be the case with true wisdom doesn't it?

It is because of everything that Ma Newby and the other Mothers have taught me, the love, respect and care they have shown me, that I have been able to sit down and write about the good times and the bad; indeed it is they who enabled me to get through some of those tougher times.

We must never underestimate the wisdom of our Mothers!

So, here are (some of) The Mothers and their teachings:

Ma Newby, my Mum

If there was one simple way to describe my Ma, I think it would most likely be one of the core principles with which she brought me up. Before I reveal that principle, let me explain that she never, to my memory anyway, actually taught me or told me the principle, rather it is something that has been observed from childhood up, in her everyday dealings with my family, our friends, colleagues, and random strangers she meets on the street.

If there is one thing in this life that I hope to have achieved by the time my day is done, it is to have carried out, to have lived that very same principle to the best and fullest of my and its potential.

As with so many of the best sayings, mantras, and quotes, it is beautifully short and simple:

> "If you can help, you must help"

Seven words. That is all. No pomp, no fancy vocabulary, just a simple seven word instruction. So simple that everyone could do it. Imagine if everyone who can or could help, did! How quickly the world would improve.

I'm not necessarily talking about solving the world's biggest problems, though there is a part of me that believes and hopes that it could - it is the same part of me that believes that too many of the world's seemingly big problems are considered such because it is in the interests of certain members of society to make them seem as such, so that they don't have to spend money or power to help in their resolution.

But, I am talking about this simple principle or rule of life being able to help with the smaller, day-to-day issues that face so many people. The issues that have a real short-term impact on people's lives, but that if resolved or the obstacle that they become removed, can free up time and head space to then enable those people to face and try to resolve the bigger, scarier, longer-term problems. Those problems can only, will only, be resolved if we all play our part, if we are all able to play our part.

In teaching me this principle, or perhaps it is a philosophy, Ma Newby also gave me one of the greatest gifts I have ever received: a determined awareness of self as well as the world around me. The self-awareness aspect was essential as it is only through such awareness that we can know whether or not we can help someone - the answer, usually, is that yes we can help them, but a lack of self-awareness results in our not knowing our own capabilities, and so we are left uncertain about whether we can help or not. We can always help, in some way. It is also this self-awareness that has enabled me to be honest with myself about the sort of person I am and want to be; someone who helps, whoever, whenever, wherever.

The determination aspect, is the part that enables me to continue trying to help others and myself, even when the task at hand seems insurmountable, or when the shouts and doubts of others are louder than the whispers of hope.

The only real flaw with this determined self-awareness, is that it has made me my own biggest critic, all-too-aware of my failings and flaws. However, the up side to that is that it also gives me strength and self-belief, because as well as knowing my weaknesses, I also know my strengths, abilities and skills.

That knowledge allows me to do things that I need and want to, things that others may find daunting, sometimes taking risks in the knowledge that I may fail and fall flat on my face, but aware that I have the strength (and support of family & friends) to get up, dust myself off, and try again.

The only way in which we truly fail is if we do not try in the first place.

It is that self-awareness and self-belief that has enabled this book to be written.

There are countless other lessons that Ma Newby has taught me during the almost thirty one years I've been her son, but this selfless act of helping others simply because you can, is probably the most powerful and most important of them all, and it is certainly one that has been a driving force in my life. That said, there is one other Ma Newby philosophy that I consider to be a fantastic tool for the journey that is life, and that, is the importance of trusting your instincts, listening to your 'gut', and wearing your heart on your sleeve.

The first two are basically the same thing for me since my instincts are closely tied to my heart, and how I feel about someone or something - again, tied directly into my self-awareness. The last one, wearing your heart on your sleeve, is something that comes naturally to some but seems impossible to fathom yet alone do, to others.

It takes a fair bit of courage to wear your heart on your sleeve, not least because you are openly displaying yourself, your thoughts, feelings and beliefs to others, but because in doing so, you are opening yourself up to criticism and hurt by those who either disagree with what you are saying, or are simply uncomfortable with the act of being so openly, unashamedly honest about how you feel.

It still amazes me that so many people get freaked out by my honesty about how I feel about a situation or a person, especially if it is them, even when I have chosen my words carefully, painstakingly so. Sadly, I think the world has grown accustomed to people keeping their true feelings to themselves, to feeling one thing but saying another for fear of looking and/or feeling stupid or in the minority - something that has never really bothered me - there's that self-awareness and self-assuredness again.

Surely that hiding of our true feelings about the things that really matter to us, weakens us and our position, as it can have a direct impact on the way in which we and those around us react to situations - since they may be based on a lie, mistruth, or simply a lack of knowledge or experience caused by this self-censorship? A Doctor can only really help someone who tells them the truth.

Wearing my heart on my sleeve has, at times, caused a lot of hurt, or rather the hurt has been caused by the actions and reactions of people with whom I have shared that heart and those feelings and beliefs. But, it is also the honesty and openness of having my heart so firmly embroidered on my sleeve, that has enabled me to get over, argue or take action against those people and their reactions. Indeed, as you would have already read, it was one such situation that drove me to write this book. Heart on sleeve works, as long as you are aware that there are some who will not appreciate it.

For all these things and more, thanks Ma. x

Binkie Robinson, my Nan

My nan, Binkie, has been a force of nature in my life for as long as I can remember. She is immediately behind Ma Newby on the list, when it comes to principles and having a direct, observable impact and influence on my life. Like Ma Newby, I have never once doubted her love for me, nor mine for her, just as (again like Ma) I have never doubted that she has my best and truest interests at heart in all she does for and says to me.

There is one principle that, when I think of Binkie immediately comes to mind, it is something I first saw when I was about 13, shortly after I started staying at her and my grandad's house on most weekends. She would come home from work, tired and frustrated. The work was ok, she seemed to quite enjoy it most of the time, the people were ok too, some were even a good laugh and easy to work with, the problem was the management.

The management's problem was that Binkie was the trade union representative, and as such there wasn't a chance that they were going to get away with their questionable practices, not just because what they were doing had a direct impact on her, but more so because it had an impact on all of them, especially some of the younger, less-vocal among them.

I quickly learnt through her actions and the letter drafting that was occasionally part of my weekend stay, that while it was important to defend yourself and your own position, it was just as important to defend others and theirs, especially those who felt that they were voiceless.

This defence of others was based, not on a need to be liked by them or even as a by-product of protecting herself, but on a need and desire for fairness and justice for all, for every single person who worked with her to be treated equally and professionally, regardless of gender, creed or colour - or, in fact, any other attribute or characteristic that may have set them apart from the majority.

I had always known that we should treat others fairly, and as equals, there was no 'regardless of...' bit, we simply treat others the same way we would like to be treated by them. As a child, I remember sticking up for a friend when someone was picking on him simply because he was a bit of geek - his geekiness was the reason we were friends; we had our own 2 member club, with a logo, and we would spend free time in lessons drawing ever more complicated video game levels on sheets of A4 paper, and coming up with different characters and powers for them, yes, I too was (and still largely am) a massive geek.

However, the defence of a friend in childhood is more of

an instinctive reaction, I didn't care if what they were doing was right (which it obviously was not), he was my friend, and as such I would defend him. What my nan was doing was a much more noble thing, though she would argue that there is nothing noble about it because it is simply the right thing to do, something everyone should do if the need arises.

It was that moment, perhaps partly due to the timing - the recent and surprising breakup of my parents coinciding with my entering adolescence, and as such a phase of constant questioning and pondering, that I really started looking at what was going on around me, not just in my immediate world of family and close friends, but the wider picture, the issues facing the world, facing the people of the world, our people, our world.

It quickly became apparent to me that there was as much injustice and inequality in the world as there was their counterparts justice and equality, but being a thirteen year old boy in a Catholic High School in Colindale, it didn't seem there was a lot I could do. So, I did what I could, I joined the School Council and the School Mentoring Programme, and I helped defend what I considered to be right and just, even when those I was helping were people I didn't know or didn't like.

This principle would form part of my core adult being, taking me to the streets of London in protests against cuts to services - this time defending a belief and the workers who work to save lives and to educate our children, too often without any real or sincere recognition from politicians. To the Conference Room of a School where I was a Governor and then Chair of Governors, defending the School, our ethos and our fantastically talented and experienced staff from the incompetence and meddling of external advisors and hacks, as well as the then Head whose idiotic, nasty, and seriously questionable actions reaffirmed my belief in the need to stand and be counted, to stand up for what and who you believe in, and not to rest until your defence was done and the day won. To ensure that when everyone else has lost their voice or the strength to speak, that you still have yours and will continue to speak until you achieve what you and they need and deserve.

All of this from simply observing and talking to my nan. My brilliant, noble, righteous-fighter of a nan.

Jane Gregg, my Friend, Mentor and former Deputy Head

My first memory of Jane was as Mrs Gregg, my nursery school Deputy Head. I remember as a child thinking that she had a nice smiley face and long shiny hair. I remember her enthusiasm for singing, sing-song, and sitting talking to children about what they liked to do. I also remember a slight cheekiness to her, that glint in the eye that you see every once in a while, and that, if you're fortunate enough, you get to see over and over again in the eyes of a friend.

I am fortunate enough.

As I grew up and went to primary, then high school, I spent a lot of time back at my nursery school - where my Mum worked and where I would go before and after school. I pretty much had free reign of the school, partly because I was well brought up so was never any trouble (except for once when I fell in to the iced-over pond, but that was entirely unintentional!), and partly because most of the staff had known me from the age of three, so I was part of the family.

I remember spending time with Jane in her class room,

often watching as she put out books and other resources, or choreographed a wall display - usually something to do with music or art, or so my memory tells me anyway. She was always lovely to me, asking how my day had been, what I had done, what I liked, all the things someone interested in children and education would ask, but always with a warmth that I realised early on meant that she wasn't simply doing the pleasantries, she actually wanted to know.

As I got older, I spent less time at the nursery, and more time at the houses of my contemporaries, or in the pub. But, every once in a while, I would pop in to the nursery to see my old, indeed oldest, friends, have a catch up, and see how they were doing. Jane was always one of the first people I'd visit, and would greet me with a hug and that same old warm, beaming smile. A smile of familiarity and friendship. We would still talk about things I was doing at school, revision, exams, people, music, but now we would talk for ages about those things, and more, both actively interested in the other's thoughts and feelings.

During my time at school, primary and high, I became hugely interested in creative writing, spending hours of my own time at home writing stories - usually adventures with a slight horror or fantasy twist, or storylines for video games. My interest in and eventual love of creative writing was nurtured by several people, including some truly outstanding English Teachers (Mr & Mrs Frayne, Mr Thompson, and Ms Ellinsworth - thank you all!), family members, and Jane.

Shortly after leaving college, I started work at the nursery school - having decided that university wasn't for me, not yet anyway. One of my duties was the typing up and tabulation of plans for all of the teachers and nursery nurses, but especially Jane who did not get on with IT - she once looked at the Staff Room clock and it stopped, never to tick again. Honestly, that actually happened, and earnt her the nickname: Mrs Ata (Ata meaning: Anti-Tech-Aura)

It was while typing up one such plan, that the idea for, or rather first two lines of a poem came into my head. I wrote them down on a pad, I always have a pad (paper or digital) with me, and carried on working. Soon, the next two lines were in my head, then the next two, then the last, and soon everything in between. I don't know where that poem came from, or why it came at that point in time during that task, but it did - perhaps the ease of the task allowed my mind to wander, but there it was, my first complete, non-academically-assigned poem.

I was very excited, not just because of the achievement of completing a poem, but because I loved what I had written - it is, to this day, still one of my favourite poems (by me). I heard about a poetry competition on the internet, and being confident with it, I submitted my poem. I didn't win, but I didn't care. Yes, it would have been awesome to win, but there I was entering poetry competitions, confident in my writing, in what I could produce. Something I had never entirely felt about my writing before that point.

I told Jane about the poem, who immediately wanted to hear it. So, I read it to her:

Dean Newby

Yesteryear

I know what I have to do, I have to be me,

Not the me that me hates,

But the me that didn't know.

You, the ones who didn't like me,

You didn't know me,

You'll wish you knew me now.

Yesteryear doesn't follow me,

It's gone,

Gone for good.

Those tears I cried,

They were for us,

But you didn't come back,

You wouldn't.

Too much pain,

Too much hurt,

I'd do it all again,

To hold you once more.

17 Pieces

You don't recognise me,

I am not the me of yesteryear,

I am not the me that you knew,

I am the me that is me.

Today, I stand with pride and a smile,

Yesteryear, I just stood.

So, drop the guises,

And rise with me,

For we are the people,

Not those of yesteryear,

But those of now.

She was silent. Thinking. Then, she stood upright, hugged me, and told me something that I have never forgotten, and try to do on a daily basis.

"Yes, you have to stay true to yourself. Do what makes you happy, what makes you smile. Definitely carry on writing poetry."

Those words, like so many ideas and philosophies in life seem simple enough, we should always stay true to ourselves, if only not to become exhausted with being the other non-us person we have created to fill some societal category or tick box. We should always try to do what makes us happy, as long as it isn't detrimental to ourselves or others, and we should definitely smile as much and as often as we can! As for the writing of poetry, I try to write as often as possible, sometimes it is poetry, sometimes prose, sometimes it can't and doesn't decide what it is until several months after it has been written, but at least it was written, and I think that is the important part of that advice.

As simple as those words and sentiments are, it was the first time in memory that anyone had said them so directly to me, and as a group of interlinked ideas. I think it no coincidence that some of the times that I smile most broadly are when I am writing a poem or a piece of prose, when I am entirely in the Writing Zone, engrossed in what I am doing, often unable to write fast enough to keep up with my thoughts as they flow from my mind to my hand. Energised and excited.

That "Definitely carry on writing poetry" line was instrumental in my writing for the next three or four years, the height of my poetry writing so far. I would write because even though I liked my first poem and thought it brilliant (it's a fine line between confidence and arrogance, isn't it?!) I was aware that others might not, and so should have something else to show them. But, Jane did like that poem, and it turned out that others did and do too - I've had school teachers who I don't know, request to use my poems in lessons, messages from strangers telling me that a poem of mine had helped them through something or touched them on a spiritual level. It's a pretty amazing feeling to have someone tell you such a thing.

In every poem and in everything I write, I stay true to myself and what makes me happy - if I don't, what I write is simply tripe, utter rubbish not worthy of the time of others.

Thank you for that gift Mrs. Ata x

Sharon Kalsi, my 'Surgo-Ma' and Early Years Enforcer

Sharon, or Shazzer as I like to call her, is one of those people who it feels like I have known my entire life, like she has always been there. Granted we have now known each other for around twenty years, but it is more than that, she is as much a member of my family as any blood relative is, she is, in fact, like an aunt to me. A crazy, funny, loving aunt.

I don't remember when her other nickname, Surgo-Ma (and her's for me: Surgo-Son) came into existence, but they are definitely representative of our relationship and feelings for each other. There are many ways and events through which our relationship can be described, but for me one of the most obvious ones and that which also shows her close relationship with Ma Newby, is this:

Twelve years ago, I got a call from Ma who was on holiday with my stepdad in Ireland. They had been in a car accident, in which their car was forced off the road and into a ditch, they were injured but not seriously. When I got off the phone with Ma, the first person I called was Shazzer. I am still not entirely sure why, it was a hugely instinctual act, but I knew that I had to tell her and that she would help in any way that she could.

Help, she did. She listened as I, a little panicked and shocked, spoke at lightning fast speed, questioning what I should do, what I could do to help - again, Ma and my stepdad were fine, but the shock of it, and all the awful ideas and images of what could have happened were sending my mind and need to help, into absolute overdrive.

Dean Newby

Shazzer was, as she so often is in those sorts of situations, calm and rational, with the warmth only a true friend can bring in times of panic and fear. She talked me through the situation, reassuring me that Ma was OK, letting me know that she would come round to the flat if I wanted or needed her to, then onto the more practical nature of things like whether or not I had enough money - Ma and my stepdad would have to stay in Ireland longer than expected, and I wasn't yet earning (it was the summer that I had finished my A-Levels)

By the time we had finished our phone conversation, I felt a whole lot better about the situation. That reassurance and comfort can only come from a true, loving friend.

That, is Shazzer.

Not only has Shazzer taught me lessons on what it is to be a good friend, especially in adulthood, she has also taught me about and is responsible for my love and commitment to education and the education system, specifically Early Years education.

I was 11 or 12 when Shazzer started working at the nursery school, my nursery school. She was the teacher of one of the classes, working alongside her nursery nurse Gabriella, and between them they would come to represent everything an outstanding Early Years team should be.

They both worked from the same ethos of putting the children front and centre in their education, making them and their interests the core part of their learning experience, and making the experience itself the key to unlocking progress and identifying the needs of every individual child who walked through their door.

This was many, many years before Government hacks were throwing terms like 'individualised, personalised learning' around. This was something that they, Shazzer and Gabriella, as Early Years practitioners and people who cared about both the work they were doing and the children they were doing it with, knew and practiced every day.

I remember once listening to Shazzer as she and other staff, it was common for teachers and nursery nurses alike to be in each other's class rooms at the end of the day, talked about the importance of a good Early Years education. She talked about Early Years being the foundation layer of education for every child fortunate enough to have one, that by doing the work early on in a child's life all education that followed could and would be able to stand firm upon the skills and knowledge learnt from the experiences of their Early Years education.

It was during this discussion that I first heard two terms that so wonderfully sum up good Early Years practice:

'awe and wonder' - that sense and feeling you get when you experience something for the first time, it is that 'Wow!' factor, seeing, hearing, feeling, tasting, experiencing something new and exciting, beginning to realise that there are things you have not yet experienced, that there is a bigger world out there for you to explore.

'learning through play' - usually how 'awe and wonder' is achieved. The act of playing and whilst doing so picking up valuable skills and gleaning pieces of knowledge from your experiences. The play is usually structured (which is very, very different to 'directed play') in a way that enables learners of various aptitudes to take different paths to different learning outcomes and objectives, all while taking into account not only the child's developmental level, but also their interests - a child who likes building is much more likely to be open to counting building blocks while they play, than they are to being called over to a table to count random animals or the like.

That was the first time anyone had so succinctly and passionately explained it to me. I had known through seeing how much the children enjoyed coming to nursery, and observing their progress throughout the year, that what was happening and being done at the nursery was clearly working, and that was no mean feat, since that year between three and four years old must be the biggest and most demanding year of developmental progress that we expect from our children, starting with tears and tantrums, and ending with them being confident, happy learners.

Shazzer is also the first teacher I remember who actively encouraged parents to play a part in their child's education, taking the time to explain what they had been doing over the day or week, ways in which they could reinforce things that had been learnt, and identifying both strengths and weaknesses, things they liked and disliked. Parents would in turn, having realised that Shazzer was obviously committed to their child, take extra time and make an extra effort to see Shazzer and have those discussions.

Something else I learnt from Shazzer, or that was at least reinforced by her, was the importance of standing your ground even in the face of true and utter adversity. There were times when she was the only one prepared to openly voice her opposition to attempts to change Early Years practice for the worse (she has never stood in the way of change, only bad change). She would also poke holes in and point out the many, and so very obvious, flaws in the latest 'recommendations' or Government initiative, knowing all too well that it would soon be replaced by another anyway.

Her decision to stand her ground and keep fighting the good fight in the knowledge that if she didn't, the battle on our home front may be lost, is something I always keep with me. It serves as a reminder that when you believe in something, truly know it to be right, you have to stand up for it, no matter the cost, because if you, who so fully believes in it doesn't defend it, who will?!

It is because of Shazzer, and others such as Gabriella, Jane and the fantastic Val Kotzen (my nursery school Headteacher and the person who employed both Ma and Shazzer), that I will always defend good Early Years practice and its practitioners against those who would seek to destroy or change it by trying to make it more directed and adult-led, less about the child and more about national averages and quotas, with more formal assessment and even more ridiculous tick box exercises - of which there are already far too many.

Shazzer, I am in awe of you, your ethos, and the work you do. Thank you x

J.G, my former Boss and Champion

I met J.G while working as an ICT Outreach Technician for a local college. She was the Headteacher of the first school I would work in following my leave of absence from work after my grandad's death.

We hit it off straight away, there was something instantly familiar and likeable about her, soon I would come to realise that it was that she and my grandad shared a very similar outlook on life - neither suffering fools gladly or having time for people who beat about the bush. She was also interested in people's lives, their stories and experiences, and what they had to offer the world, and her

Dean Newby

school.

What I learnt from J.G in our six and half years of working together, or rather my working for her school, and her, frustrated when IT didn't do what she wanted, asking if we could replace it all with blackboards and chalk, was that while it is important and correct to expect others to treat you as you would them, it is just as important to realise that they may not do so, but that you must, in both personal and professional situations and settings, continue to. The true loser of an argument is he who loses his temper and forgets his manners, for when he does, all people hear are the shouts, not the words.

This was something I already knew, but her guidance and actions, and my observations of such actions during that time, especially those that revolved around me, cemented my belief in the need for unwavering personal and professional courtesy and civility.

This lesson was most directly taught, much to the chagrin of two of my detractors, quite openly and directly, and both in circumstances that, were I proved to be in the wrong, could have meant the loss of my main client and livelihood. The first was when, having treated an external company with nothing but professional respect and courtesy, they tried to blame me for something going wrong, and files being lost. Now, I am far too honest and ethically-minded a person to lie about such a thing, I would have gone straight to J.G and told her, had it happened on my watch, just as I am far too good at my job and what I do to allow such a thing to happen. J.G knew this, and so having asked them a few questions, including the time and date of when the error occurred and as such catching them in a lie (I was off-site, they were on-site), she ordered them off the school premises.

17 Pieces

The second such example was over a simple miscommunication between myself and a trainer who was coming in to the school to deliver an ICT inset day to the staff. Everything the trainer had said they needed had been pre-installed, configured and tested. However, upon arriving at the school the trainer found that a piece of software they needed for the training, had not been installed.

I was summoned to J.G's office with the then ICT Co-ordinator for a meeting, whereupon the trainer proceeded to have a go at me. I kept repeating my point, that the list I had been given didn't contain the resource and so it wasn't installed, the entire time being professional - though indignant and incensed by the rudeness I was subjected to. Eventually, I had to ask the trainer to change their tone, stating that while they had been quite rude and unprofessional, overstepping the mark and barking orders as if they were my boss (and even my boss wouldn't be permitted to speak to me in such a way), I had remained calm and professional. When the trainer continued their barrage, I turned to J.G, shutting the trainer out and signalling that I had said all there was to say, and was not going to let this continue for much longer.

J.G told the trainer that while she and I were clearly sorry that they didn't have everything they needed to deliver the training to its fullest (though, I noted, they had somehow still managed to teach the staff everything they needed to know), they, the trainer, had neglected to include the resource on the list, and so how was I to know that it was needed. The trainer was stunned. I was vindicated and victorious.

Soon after each of those experiences, J.G called me into her office to congratulate me on remaining professional when I was not being treated the same way, at all. I remember her remarking that it took incredible self-belief to be able to do so, and to continue doing so even in the most heated of arguments. I replied that it wasn't easy, but I had both truth and righteousness on my side. She loved that, always being a fan of those who stood their ground when right - disliking those who did so when wrong, time wasters and troublemakers.

J.G was also probably the first Headteacher to recognise that I wasn't the stereotypical IT Technician. I actually have interpersonal skills, and am able to get on with and effectively communicate with pretty much anyone, and more than that, that those skills are one of my stronger skills sets. That, matched with a strong work ethic, honesty, and a directness that I know (because she told me) she found refreshing, would play a key part in her school being my first client upon leaving my job at the college and setting up my own IT Support Business.

Those two things alone, the philosophy of remaining civilised and courteous even when under attack or not being treated the same way, and her having faith and belief in me and my abilities, and therefore coming on board as my first client, are what make J.G my Champion.

One last thought on these and the other Mothers...

The combined lessons and direct experience of having these and other Mothers in my life, about four years ago, led to the creation of a personal mantra that, though is sometimes difficult to fully embrace - on the days when my path seems less clear, is nonetheless something I still grip hold of:

ADAHAB

Always Dream
Always Hope
Always Believe

Dean Newby

7 / 17
ONE EYE ON THE GROUND

As often happens in life, a confluence of events - my grandad retiring, my parents separating, and my entering adolescence, meant that my grandad and I were there for each other at a time when each of us needed someone.

He needed a friend, a pal to spend time with during the day while my nan was out at work.

I needed a friend, a confidante to whom I could talk about anything and know that they would be there for me.

I had always loved my grandad, but it wasn't until that point in time, when our paths intertwined in an entirely inseparable way that I started to love him because of him, the person he was, not just because of my hereditary grandad-grandson link to him.

Soon, I loved him as more than a grandad. He had become and even now, 9 years after his death, continues to be one of the best friends I've ever had.

Dean Newby

On the night that my grandad died, as everyone left the hospital room, I stayed behind to say my own goodbye. I took his hand and promised to pass his lessons and stories on to those in the family who hadn't heard them or were yet to be born into the family. Then I kissed him on the forehead and left the room.

Over the next few weeks, especially in the lead up to his funeral, I set about writing notes about his stories to enable me to properly and accurately retell them. The process of doing that was such a catharsis, instead of being grief-stricken I was laughing at his stories, the implausibility of some of them, how some of them got more dramatic with each retelling, and the memories we'd made as he retold them, walking to the shops, sitting in the garden, just being there for and with each other.

I believe that all people have something to teach, and in turn we all have something we can learn from each person. Where my grandad is concerned, that is most definitely the case, and while some of his lessons were taught implicitly and through direct experience, others were taught in his uniquely direct way - one of the things I've always respected most about him.

In a similar vein to his stories, these are all lessons that people deserve to hear, so here are 9 of my favourites.

Lesson #1 -
Never mess about with another man's woman
...or water!

The first part of this lesson, or rule, was something I remember grandad saying on more than one occasion, it doesn't need explanation, it is what it is.

However, the water part was tacked on by him later. I remember standing in the kitchen with him and one of my uncles, I was probably 14 or so. My uncle flicked some water at me, so I did the same to him - this sort of thing was common in our family, often being instigated by grandad. I don't know if we splashed my grandad, or if he just didn't want us doing it, but he put himself in between us, arms out in a 'calm down' position, and said: "You never mess about with water! Never mess about with another man's woman...or water!" He wasn't telling us off as such, just letting us know that we should stop.

Later on, as we sat in the back room I asked if he meant we should never mess about with water, or with another man's water...he looked at me, smiled and replied: "Cheeky little fucker!" and we laughed.

Lesson #2 - Say Hello!

My grandad always showed and told me that above all else you should be polite, mannerly. He was also interested in people, and felt it important to stop and take the time to talk to them. So we did.

Whenever we went on one of our walks to the corner shop or further into Harrow Weald, he would say "Morning" to everyone we passed, everyone. He'd often accompany it with a nod or tip of the head and a slight eyebrow raise. More often than not they would reciprocate, the ones who didn't becoming his next objective - he always, in the end, got them to say hello.

But, before we even got halfway up the road we would have stopped at least once to talk to one of the older ladies who would be out in their front gardens caring for their flowers and hedges. He called them his 'girlfriends' - something my

nan & I took great joy in winding him up about!
A 25 minute round trip to the corner shop would usually end up being closer to an hour, but it was always worth it, if only to hear him tell his stories or offer his advice on how to save their roses.

He once best summed it up with a one-liner, yet another of his talents: "There's always time to say 'Hello'"

Lesson #3 - The Art of Sandwich Making

This was something that my grandad felt very strongly about, to him the order in which you made the sandwich had a direct impact on how it tasted. His formula was simple, though still seems a little strange to me:

- Butter both slices of bread...

- Slice the cheese and place it on the right hand slice, any offcuts to be eaten immediately - Take a good dollop of sandwich pickle and roughly spread it over the cheese (not the other slice of bread!)

- Place the left slice of bread on top of the cheese & pickle, gently press down

- Cut into two triangles

Now, I've tried it that way and my own way, I can't really tell a difference...except I have a lot more pickle on mine and it's spread on the bread edge to edge, corner to corner (like the butter)

However, the more important lesson to take away from this is the sandwich's accompaniment, its side, and that should, must always be a good packet of crisps. A sandwich without crisps is a naked sandwich, half a sandwich, half a lunch! Grandad, without fail, always had a 6 pack of cheese & onion crisps in the cupboard, and in that brilliant way that grandparents do, there was always a packet of salt & vinegar for me.

Lesson #4 -
Just try it, if you don't like it, don't do it, but try

It's a simple lesson or idea, but to a teenager, feeling a little lost in the world, it was an eloquent reassurance. It implied that everything would be ok if I tried and either failed or didn't like what I experienced, while emphasising the importance of at least trying, experiencing something new.

Now, this was something Ma taught me from a very early age, that you should try everything unless you really, really don't want too or don't feel safe doing it. She also taught that whatever you do or try to do, you do with all the effort you can muster.

So, while my grandad was reiterating Ma's longheld belief & lesson, that additional person willing me on to try new things, try stepping out of my comfort zone, was an incredible source of strength when doing just that.

Lesson #5 - Life is like a hand outstretched

'Hand Out'

A hand outstretched

At the end of each finger

Another hand outstretched

Dean Newby

Hands, spanning the path

From Birth to Death

Each palm a question or event

Each finger an answer or action

Each decision,

Leading to another palm

Leading to another question

The choices made

The path created

That poem was inspired by one of the greatest lessons my grandad ever taught me, not just that life is a series of questions or events that we must answer or react to, but that there is often more than one answer or option available to us, we just have to know to look and be open to the possibility that some of the options may not seem like options at all, at first.

Because of these teachings and the life I've experienced since then, I've always thought of life's choices as trackable, that if you sit down and think, honestly, you can track back to the bigger (and some of the smaller) events and decisions in your life, and to the point in time that you arrived at the question (or, keeping with the poem, the palm), and then the point before that and so on.

This is one of the ways in which we can learn from past mistakes, discover where exactly it was that we went wrong, and then hope and work to never make the same mistake again.

Lesson #6 - "There's only one thing in life..."

My grandad said as we stood looking through the glass on the front door, spying out onto the street, something we often did.

"...that you've got to do. And, that's die! Yep, only one thing you've got to do in life, and that's die!"

I remember being startled by his comment, on this, the first time he'd said it to me. After a moment, I asked:

"What about work?" his response: "Nah, you haven't GOT to work" "Yeah, but without work, there's no money, without that there's no home..." he looked at me: "No, but you're still breathing ain't ya?!"

I hadn't really thought about life in that way before, of course it could be argued that while you don't have to do anything in life but die, the point of life is to do things, to be something, to hopefully make a difference in the world. But, that wasn't his point. He was simply stating that while it may sometimes seem that there is something you have to do, no matter how much you don't want to, from a purely technical, literal perspective, you don't have to do it. Even if there's a gun to your head, you have a choice, you don't have to do what is being asked of you, though this may of course lead to your death, strangely fulfilling grandad's lesson.

Lesson #7 - Know how to take the piss
...out of yourself.

This was a lesson that grandad really hammered home. He was aware, as grandparents often are, without my ever mentioning it, that I was having a hard time at school. I had found myself in the crosshairs of a boy who, for whatever reason, didn't like me. He would shout cruel, horrible things at me on the bus, push me out of the way, all that sort of thing, and I put up with it for quite a while. But, it was getting to me.

My grandad, without once referencing my having a hard time at school or anything even related to that, probably because he knew I'd get defensive and would therefore not really hear his point, told me that to get through life you have to be able to take the piss out of yourself, to laugh at your ineptitude and failings, to show that actually you know that you aren't good at 'x', or were fatter than most people, or lived in Harlesden...teenagers have such a strange view of what a good put-down is!

Then came the most telling line of this piece of advice, which I've embraced as a lesson: "...because if you take the piss out of yourself, and get there before they can, there's nothing they can say! They'd be repeating what you've already said, and make themselves look like a fucking idiot!"

Now, this came as an absolute revelation to me. I adopted it straight away, and strangely I very quickly became popular because of it, or at least because of the confidence, all of it a facade, it conveyed to my peers. Teenagers are so insecure that for one of us to point out our own shortcomings and laugh at them, more than that, try to get others to laugh at them with us and deliver them in a 'Yeah, I know, what an idiot!' style, must mean that that person is full of confidence and doesn't give a toss what people think - something else I soon adopted, and still to this day practice.

That false confidence was definitely the starting point for what would soon become a real, truer, fuller confidence, one where I could speak in a self-assured manner, confident in my opinions and comfortable with myself, a manner which would then give rise to the person I am today. But, I still take the piss out of myself, seeing it now as more of a strength of character, of true confidence, because now I do it, not in defence, but as recognition and self-awareness of my flaws, something I think every person could do with knowing about themselves.

Lesson #8 - Dratsab

Ressot (Ress-ott)
Reknaw (Reck-nor)
Dratsab (Drat-sab)
Rekcuf (Reck-uff)
Tnuc (Tee-nook)

These are all examples of the backslang (and pronunciation) my grandad so gleefully taught me when I was 13, taking the time to ensure I pronounced each of them correctly. The learning of backslang isn't a life lesson per se, but it is a lesson in breaching 'the norms of society', of being your own person and doing your own thing. How many grandad's do you know who teach their grandchildren not just how to swear, but how to do it backwards?

Grandad was, in some ways, a traditionalist, but in a whole lot of other ways he was far from it, choosing instead to carve out his own brilliantly hilarious, caring, loving, direct image, or at least that's what he showed me and how I saw him - we do after all, all show different people different sides of ourselves.

I think I probably saw one of the truer sides of him, possibly an advantage of the grandchild-grandad relationship, not having to be the primary worrier, caregiver (lookerafterer, as he would have called it), instead being able to enjoy everything, have the mental worry-less space to enjoy everything, and therefore the time to enjoy being together.

Another of his less-traditional-grandad sayings was something he picked up while doing his National Service. He and his fellow servicemen would be awoken by the shouting of: "'ands off cocks, and on with socks!" I first learnt of this when, one morning, grandad walked into my bedroom shouting the same thing while banging the bottom of a sweet tin, immediately bursting into laughter at his own cruelty and probably my more than startled reaction.

There was, of course, a cup of tea waiting for me downstairs, once I'd got my socks on.

Lesson #9 - One eye on the ground

Once, while walking to the corner shop, my grandad spotted a coin on the floor, bent and picked it up then put it in his pocket. "Always keep one on the ground" he said as we continued our walk.

A few months later, while on another trip to the corner shop, we walked, both of us with one eye on the ground. As we passed through 'the shortcut', a small area of muddy grassland with a few trees that joins my nan & grandad's road to a point in the main road that's closer to the shops, I spotted something half hidden under a leaf. Upon bending down to pick it up, I discovered that it was a beautiful green fountain pen, heavy, cold in my hand.

I excitedly showed it to my grandad; finally I'd found something worth picking up! He took it in his hand and examined it, then, without missing a beat, put it in his pocket, to "keep it safe" for me.

I never saw that pen again. Clearly, the other part of this lesson was "and the other eye on your companion"

The pen, or rather its disappearance, would become a long-running joke between the two of us, something we were still laughing about years later. But, I never did see that pen again.

Never take life too seriously, laugh whenever you can, spend time with those you love, swear and swear well, think before you act - but do act, be polite to everyone...and if all that fails, make a good sandwich.

Those are just a handful of the things my grandad taught me, and it is because of those, the man he was and the way he was with me, that I, in times when I'm not sure how I feel or what I think about something, ask one thing: what would grandad say or do?!

Dean Newby

8 / 17
IN SAFE HANDS

Dear Mon Oncle, I was writing about the family recently, in part for the family tree, in part for my book.

I started writing down some of my memories of you, of us, and soon came to realise that there was a common theme that ran through them. Safety. The fact that I have, for as long as I can remember, always felt safe with you, I've always known, somehow, that you have my back. So, I thought I'd send you some of my memories that show that, because what's the point in having them and feeling them if I then don't share them?!

So, while words cannot express how truly thankful I am for having you in my life, and this from someone who, as you know, is a firm believer in the power and strength of words, I hope my memories at least show a little of what you have meant and do mean to me x
'In Safe Hands' - Memories of Mon Oncle.

So often, love is expressed through actions, some out of the ordinary, most through everyday occurrences, or simple,

Dean Newby

little-thought things we do for those we love.

This, I assume is where 'actions speak louder than words' comes from, and while actions do and can 'speak' very loudly, I have always believed that words can speak just as loudly, if not more so, as long as you know how to use them.

Mon Oncle is someone who is skilled in both actions and words of love, and I've been fortunate enough to experience both, personally, many times.

The first memory (of three) of Mon Oncle and me, is this: I'm not sure how old I was, but I think I was about 7. Me, Mon Oncle and Ma had been up talking in my nan and grandad's back room, it was a Friday night - I still remember the sound of various late night Friday TV shows on in the background. At some point during the conversation I fell asleep, but I remember bits of muddled conversations, hushed tones, and that semi-whisper used only in late night conversation - dry whispers with an occasional cracked dry word.

I was still in this state of semi-sleep when Mon Oncle lifted me from the sofa in one smooth, effortless motion. I don't remember consciously deciding not to open my eyes, but I didn't. Instead, I let him carry me from the back room, up the stairs, and into my bedroom. It may seem strange to some that I have dedicated one and a half paragraphs to this one simple moment, but it was one of the times in my life that I felt entirely safe. Not to say that I felt unsafe at other times, but it was a conscious recognition of safety, of feeling like I was untouchable.

In that moment, Mon Oncle had conveyed his love for me, his young nephew.

17 Pieces

We spend a lot of time celebrating the BIG events in and of life, and it is right that we do so. But, it is also right that we celebrate the smaller ones too, even if only on an individual, personal level.

The second memory of this piece, happened shortly before my thirteenth birthday. I was staying at my nan and grandad's house for a week during the summer holidays. Mum came a day earlier than planned because she and my Dad had broken up the previous evening, and obviously she needed to tell me and the rest of the family. I was actually pretty ok with it really, even then I was very much aware that I had never had any sort of real relationship with my Dad, we had little in common, he worked a lot of nights, and when he was home he wasn't really present or proactive in spending time with me, so there wasn't really anything to miss. I was also, and probably still am, a bit of a Mummy's Boy - we've always had more in common than most, and above all else she spent time with me, often doing things I enjoyed. She made an effortless effort.

The day after my Mum's early, post-breakup arrival, Ma went to see Mon Oncle and his wife, to tell them the news.

It wasn't very long until Mon Oncle was on the phone to me at my nan's house, telling me that we were going to Harrow for lunch and comic book perusal (he almost certainly didn't say 'perusal', but it works), and that he was on his way to pick me up. Soon enough he was at the front door, and we made our way to the bus stop.

I don't remember the actual discussions that took place on the bus to Harrow, but rather the sentiment of 'I'm here for you' with a lot of jokey, mocking stuff thrown in for good measure - as is our way. I've found over time that the words used by others, are often replaced, in memory, by their sentiment and purpose. The most profound feeling I got from that day, something I still carry with me, is that he had and still has my back.

Things change when you become consciously aware of the support and back-having of another, wherever they are. Indeed, at the risk of sounding like a complete nutcase, in times of strife, sadness or disillusionment, when I have come across a seemingly insurmountable obstacle, I have visualised my entire family standing behind me, stony-faced with arms crossed firmly across their chests - a picture of defiance and determination, righteousness and strength, indignant and enraged by whatever issue has crossed my path, their hearts and minds willing me forward, unto the breach of whatever issue has arisen.
It may sound a little on the dramatic side (pause for those who know me to nod in recognition), and even perhaps a little corny, but it has always worked for me.

I should point out that this image is not simply one I dreamt up, but rather is based on a real-life event, where we as a family stood together at my nan's front door, entirely as a show of strength against a neighbour who had thrown a brick over the garden fence, narrowly missing one of us.

Back to the second of three memories, perhaps Mon Oncle was simply the catalyst for a feeling that I needed at the time, perhaps he was the one who could best communicate it, or for me, personified it. Whatever it was, his again simple act of being there, of being present, has had a lasting impact on my life. I hope I am and have been there for people in the same way.

The third of three memories about Mon Oncle, is from about 4 or so years after the second, and it isn't solely his own.

17 Pieces

It was Christmas, which in our family means a month or so of continual, sustained excitement, shopping and list making, and traditions, lots and lots of traditions - our traditions! From the counting of people for the Christmas Dinner, several weeks in advance, to the checking off of present categories by my nan - we always got: a CD, an item of clothing, a book, a toy, game or gadget, and some sweets - she would go through the lists she'd made in her head, using an 'Mm' to represent the categories: "So, he's got: an Mm, an Mm, and an Mm. So I still need to get..."

We would often have Christmas Day Dinner at my nan and grandad's, followed by Christmas Day Tea at my aunty's, and Boxing Day Tea at my other aunty's, eating and drinking more than anyone should over any two day period, often needing a nap, but being too excited to have one - I still, at 30, get very excited by Christmas and everything I do with my family and friends at that time of year.

Anyway, back to the story. Me and Ma arrived at my nan and grandad's on Christmas Eve, to be there for Christmas Day morning, and the fun of opening all of our presents - we would bring all of our unopened presents from friends and colleagues with us, resulting in what is officially called 'The Showing', where we open our presents and then show them to everyone who enters the house, whether they want to look at them or not. It's tradition.

The madness of Christmas Eve is one of my favourite things about Christmas, and this one was no different. When else in the year do you go from 'top and tailing' sprouts - something my grandad used to do over a bowl while watching the Top of the Pops 2 Christmas Special in the back room, to wrapping a present you just found in one of the pockets of a coat hanging in the cupboard in the box room (also known as the 'Present Wrapping Room', come

Dean Newby

Christmastime), to watching half a film, then putting the Turkey on, before going back to wrap another present you've just remembered you hid in the airing cupboard. As a child, I was only an observer of this organised chaos, but it is something that made me really appreciate both the enthusiasm and dedication of my nan, and the laid-back helpfulness of my grandad. I would, as an adult, adopt a similar approach to Christmas Eve, choosing to wrap presents for those I would see on Christmas morning only once the night of Christmas Eve had arrived, sometimes staying up until 2am or later to do so. It's tradition!

Night eventually welcomed day, and after the gifts were revealed and their wrapping paper hastily discarded, and with excited anticipation fulfilled, a phone call caused a little chaos. Mon Oncle had been rushed to hospital.

So, in a fashion entirely true of our family, arrangements were made, dinner was moved to my aunty's house, and I, in my new Christmas clothes, clambered into the back of an uncle's van, cooked Turkey - still hot in its oven tray, fat 'n' all, held firmly on my lap, and off we went to my aunty's, while my nan and grandad went to the hospital to visit Mon Oncle.

Our Christmas traditions continued as they should, and we got on with the day as our family usually did when such moments arose, eating, laughing, enjoying each other's company. Perhaps the hugs were a little closer that day, and all of us listened carefully when the phone rang, awaiting news of Mon Oncle. It finally came, he was ok, tests needed to be done, but he would be ok, we could all rest a little more easily.

We went to my other aunty's on Boxing Day, as was the tradition, the family pulling closer together, making more of an effort - now, my family is a very close one, I and most of my cousins grow up around each other, we see each other for birthdays and pretty much any other celebration you can think of, and often in between, but that Christmas, we all felt a little closer than in previous ones. We all went out of our way to make it easier, calmer for my nan and grandad, aunts and uncles, all of us taking a little more time to appreciate one another.

Mon Oncle phoned to wish us a Merry Christmas, and we each in turn spoke to him. I, of course, called him an attention seeker - that sort of mocking and banter being a core factor of our relationship and friendship, but I remember as we were about to hang up, having an overwhelming need to tell him that I loved him, so I did. Strangely enough, for someone I am so close to, and as someone who has always told my Ma that I love her, even when just going out for the night, or hanging up the phone, I think that was probably the first time I'd ever told Mon Oncle that! That was the moment that I started telling those I was close to, those I loved, that I loved them.

I think *that* Christmas showed something that most of us already knew, that together we make for one hell of a strong family, that we are there for one another in good times and in bad. Indeed, shortly after, a good friend of mine came to a cousin's birthday party, and having spent an hour or so with us, said the following - I am paraphrasing:

...your family are something else! Dean, I'm Italian, we get 'family', but yours is more than that, it's friendship too...

I think that quite nicely and accurately sums up both us as a family, and my relationship with Mon Oncle.

Dean Newby

9 / 17
LOVE…?!

Frank sat, quietly, peacefully in the back room of his house, sunbeams dancing through the crack in the curtains, highlighting specks of floating dust. He loved days like this, the warm beat of the sun only being interrupted by the slightest of breezes, carrying upon them the sweet smells of summer.

With his eyes closed, he found his mind wandering through the streets of time that were his life, a childhood of bombed out houses and trips to family in the north, the street that led him to his wife, the various jobs, the births of all his children, the streets those children walked and the streets their children, his grandchildren walked.

On this particular summer's afternoon, his mind took a left turn down the street so far walked by his grandson, Paul.

Before Paul was even born, Frank knew they'd have a special bond. He would be, after all, the son of Frank's little girl, his baby, his 'chicken'.

Dean Newby

Paul entered the back room, and watched as his grandad's closed eyes flickered. "Hello you old bastard", he said in his usual tone, indicating his presence and demanding a response. "'ello ya little fucker" came Frank's whispered response, eyes still shut, a slight smile in his face.

"What are you thinking about?" asked his grandson, knowing that he would always get an honest answer. "You actually! The day we first met" said Frank, knowing only too well that Paul would reply with something along the lines of: "Oh, the greatest day of your life you mean?!" which he did. Frank's smile broadened, revealing the deep laughter lines of weathered skin around his closed eyes.

Happy with his grandad's response, Paul sat in his usual spot, opposite the window, near the door, put his hands on his lap and closed his eyes. He too loved days like this.

Frank had always liked telling a story or spinning a yarn, and most of his life's experiences were stored in his memory in that way. Tales of delivery boy exploits, going into service under a King and coming out under a Queen, Sorting Office antics, and memory after memory of he and his mates having a laugh on the building sites. But, right now, at this particular moment, he was remembering Paul, the memories they'd made so far, and the memories they had yet to make.

Paul had always loved his grandad as most children do, but just before he turned 13, something happened that would change their lives and their relationship forever. Paul's parents, one being Frank's little girl, separated and Paul spent much more time at Frank and Beryl's than he had before - it was a form of therapy for he and his Mum, she needed time to heal without having to actively worry about Paul, and Paul needed time to heal without having to actively worry about his Ma. The separation came at a time when Frank was in need of a friend too, having been recently retired due to ill health. Retirement is a cruel thing for a man so used to being in work.

It was here that Frank's memory, the street down which Paul was travelling, had split into so many other streets, so many memories of time spent together.

There was always one memory that made Frank smile, and knowing that winter would soon be coming, he let his mind wander into it.

It was almost Christmas, and Frank and Paul were walking into Harrow Weald to get some shopping for lunch. This was part of their ritual, on days when Frank's lungs could cope with the weather, they'd walk the mile to the shop then get the bus back. On days when the 'fat man' as Frank called it, was sitting on his chest, they'd get the bus both ways - Frank, and Paul, always preferred the walk.
They stopped on their way to take in the view over London, this was one of the best views Paul had ever seen, and he marveled at it every single time, observing the dip of London's basin, something Frank pointed out on each occasion, without fail.

As they reached Harrow Weald proper, Frank decided they needed to pay a trip to the local DIY store, not for anything in particular, just for a look around. As they entered, they were met by staff who didn't seem to know it was Christmas, not a smile to be seen anywhere. "Miserable fuckers", Frank's assessment of the situation, "Merry Fuckin' Christmas" Paul's response.

They wandered around the shop for a bit, looking at various non-Christmas accessories and the like, until from another aisle, Frank shouted "Pauly!!" Paul putting down the DIY Electronics Kit he'd been examining for some time now, quickly honed in on his grandad's voice and was soon by his side.

In front of them stood an entire aisle of Christmas character figures, Santa Claus, Reindeers, Snowmen, Penguins, Robins, Christmas Trees and various barely-Winter-let-alone-Christmas items, also known as pure unadulterated tat. They all seemed to have dodgy black plastic buttons or pull-cords with 'Try Me' stickered all over them. So, they did.

Paul pressed a button on the shoe belonging to some murderous looking Santa figure, at first nothing, then a terrifying sound of metal on metal, flashing eyes, and a tinny 'Jingle Bells'. Then came Frank's turn, he chose a group of Reindeer who, upon pressing a too-big switch slap bang in the middle of their podium, sang a not-bad rendition of 'Silent Night'.

It was at this point that, without discussion or even a gesture, that the pair began turning on every figure that they could, pressing every button, pulling every pull-cord, flicking every switch, all with a look of determination on their faces, a mission to be completed, a mission of supreme importance.

As they came to the end of the aisle, they looked back at what they had created, a cacophony of bells, tinny tunes and questionable voices. They looked at each other and smiled, delighted with themselves, proud even. They'd created something brilliant from an aisle of shite, as Frank would have put it.

As they left the store, Paul whistled one of the Santa figure's horrific tunes, looking sideways at his Grandad, waiting for a response. They both started laughing, one of those small, low chuckles that starts deep in the pit of your belly, then rumbles up through you, until you burst, head thrust forward, shoulders jiggling. It was a mischievous laugh, their usual laugh.

That memory, that story, would soon become one of the most told Christmas stories of all time (within their family and groups of friends, at least), each time it was told it became a little bigger, a little louder, and each and every time they both laughed just as much, if not more.
As Frank sat, his smile now wider than it had been, he thought about all the things he hoped he had taught his grandchildren, those important life lessons that he'd had to learn the hard way, he didn't want them to have it as hard as he had. He thought about those lessons, about how he'd learnt them, and then remembered something he'd decided a long time before.

It wasn't the duty of a grandparent to teach lessons, it was their duty to be there for their grandchildren, to create fun and laughter, to retell family stories, perhaps there were lessons in those that the grandchildren would themselves discover?

He still hoped, however, that he had at least instilled some sort of sense of purpose, perhaps even one or two principles, in his many grandchildren. He had ensured that whenever the opportunity arose, he used his, what had inevitably become, catchphrase: "There's only one thing you have to do in life, and that's die!" - of course, that hadn't been of much help when Paul was trying to decide on a project title for his school geography project, but Frank hoped the sentiment had.

Dean Newby

Frank's mind was growing tired, so many memories had been created over his nearly 70 years on this planet, revisiting them was so very tiring, these days most things were, but at least with his memories he could look back with pride at the life he had led, and happiness and love at the people he had in it.

Despite his tiring mind, Frank left Paul's street, and took a left onto the High Road, up ahead he could see the chicken and DIY shops, then on a little further he passed Long Elmes, and took a right onto Weald Lane, the road he lived on as a child. As he turned, the sun shone brightly in his eyes, shielding them with his hand, he pressed on, determined to see the house that was his first home.

He could hear, just beyond the end of the road, a sound, or at least the after effect of a sound. It was like several people murmuring quietly to themselves, but not quite, more like whispers or quieter still. The voices and remnants of times past, memories of other people and other times perhaps?

As he walked towards the house, he felt his lungs begin to loosen, air once again being able to fill every nook and cranny. He hadn't felt like this since he was a boy! He walked a little more, and as he approached the gate of the house, he felt someone take his hand, he didn't need to look for who it was, he knew, and as they stood in front of his first home, the sun beat warmer and brighter on his face, and he smiled.

17 Pieces

'Love...?!'

...is a husband preparing for sleep eternal,
who while even on a morphine high,
knows that the hand he holds,
if only for a brief moment,
is not the hand of his wife,
and with eyes closed,
calls her back to him

Dean Newby

10 /17
I'M COMING OUT…

Read, take a minute and let me know…

I tried so hard,

To speak my words

But at countdown's end,

My mind was blanked

Want

Perhaps a letter,

Or maybe a txt,

Perhaps a banner,

Dean Newby

Or flashing lights across my chest

Need

And so you see,

To my oldest friend, I say

Quite simply, my words;

"Ma, I'm gay"

Have

I know that I'm loved,

And that your support, I have

I know that I'm respected,

And that my back, you have

Know

Should you have questions,

Just simply ask,

And together we'll dismantle

What can seem like a mammoth task

Relief

That poem is how I came out to my Mum. It came at the end of weeks of trying to tell her, each time thwarted by a too-dry throat, palpitations, or sudden mind-blanking. I'd decided almost a year beforehand that I was going to tell her, soon, but the past few months saw my confidence build, things were going very well at work, I had my own place, and was feeling more and more secure in the world. But still I wasn't able to get the words out. Then, I went to London Pride.

I went along with two female friends from school, we stood in Trafalgar Square, drinking, enjoying the atmosphere and acts on stage, I, checking out many a man. After a while, a woman took to the stage and began telling us all a story.

It was a story of LGBT activists from her country who were 'being disappeared', suddenly and systematically disappearing after Pride events or LGBT/Equality sit-ins, never to be heard from again. She then went on to congratulate us and London for being such an accepting and open city, for being able to hold such a huge LGBT Pride Festival, and for working across Europe and beyond for equality. As I stood there, my sense of inequality and injustice inflamed and incensed by what I'd heard, such awful unjust actions being taken against innocent people, I realised that I had a duty to come out.

Now, that sense of duty is an entirely personal thing, I'm not saying anyone else should feel it or act upon it, but for me, I had no real reason not to come out. I am from a fairly liberal family, and beyond that I'm from a loving and caring family, a family that looks out for one another, and has always been there through thick and thin. So, there I was with that sense of injustice and a duty to those who couldn't come out, to be an out proud gay man, but still I had the issue of dry-throat, etc. When I got home that night, I sat down to write my Ma a letter, but that letter quickly became that poem, and what followed, the reactions and comments, would change my life forever.

Ma: when my Mum had read the poem, she gave me a call. Having told me that she loved me and that she of course had my back, she brilliantly went into rational Mum-mode and said: "I just have three questions...

What about HIV? What about Gaybashings? What about Grandchildren?" I, having not at all thought about those questions or how I would answer them, having only been focused on telling her, said the first instinctual things that came to me: "I use condoms. I'm careful when I'm out. I still want kids, nothing has changed" and that was pretty much that. I mean obviously later there were discussions about why it had taken me so long to tell her, and all of that sort of thing, but all of those discussions with her and anyone else who asked, were an absolute breeze compared to the torment I felt in those weeks of trying and failing to tell her.

Nan: When I told my Nan, her reaction was, really quite brilliantly: "Ooo, you can find a nice gay man to go dancing with!" ...followed by lots of loving, caring comments, and quite a few questions.

Aunty: When one of my aunts was told, she sent me a text message telling me how much she loved me, but the Outing-related memory I will always have of her, came a couple of years later, when during a personality-based quiz, I was asked: What are you proudest of?

In the moment, I couldn't think of anything, but my Aunt quickly and seemingly without having to think about it replied: "When you came out. You should be proud of that, you were so brave. We're still proud of you!"

Friend and boss: simply grabbed me, gave me a huge hug, and with tears in her eyes (because she felt it sad that I hadn't been able to tell anyone for so long), kept saying: "Well done!"

One of my oldest friends, and the woman who is like a Second Mother to me: started crying as soon as she saw me (standard for such events & occasions), and gave me one of those incredibly reassuring hugs, and told me she was proud of me. That's probably one of the few times I got teary - after telling Ma.

Mon Oncle: I sent him a text message to tell him as he was one of the ones I wanted to tell myself. His reply came quickly: "Ah penistouch [this would be my nickname for quite some time], good for you mate. I fully expect to see you passed out, half naked on the beaches of Brighton, surrounded by pools of your own vomit, come Brightonhog Pride. We love you x"

Friend and former-colleague: congratulated me then asked if I had a boyfriend, and where she would be in the pecking order of meeting him, should I one day get one. She, I also want to add, has always been an amazing supporter of my writing, and has always encouraged me to go after and do whatever I want to.

Cousin: having congratulated me "for liking dick", suggested that we have a competition to see who could bring to a family event, the boy that would most-freak-out the less-liberal members of our family. We still, neither of us, have really done that. Game on!

These are just a collection of some of the responses I got

when I first came out, they are the funnier or unique responses, but that shouldn't make anyone think that I didn't appreciate every single positive response I received. And there were a lot of them - all of my cousin's, who were at the time adults/or nearly so, sent me supportive and loving messages, as did all of my uncles and aunts, colleagues - then-present & former, and everyone else I felt I either needed or wanted to tell.

However, sadly, from conversations I've had with friends and fellow gays, it seems that my story and experiences are in the minority. That a large majority of people face rejection and sometimes hate, even from those who are supposed to love them unconditionally. There isn't a lot I can do about that, other than campaign for a more equal society and future - I believe such equality will eventually force light onto the ignorance of hate, and either change the minds or hearts of those would-be-haters, or make them so ashamed of that hatred, that they will force it deep within themselves and not act on it - I, of course, prefer the former.

One thing I can and still do, six years on, is celebrate the day I came out to my Ma and therefore the world. It was a hugely personal victory, and one I feel deserves celebration in its own right, but I also think that if just one person, who may be going through the turmoil I went through, or worse (with a family they are certain is going to reject them) sees my happiness and jubilation, it may just help them, even if it's only a little. And that is worth it.

The 1st of July is my Outiversary,
and it is an event I will always celebrate.

FRIENDS? FOREVER?

PIECES 11 – 14

Dean Newby

11 / 17
THE GIRLS ARE BACK IN TOWN

I have always been a girls man, in that I generally find it easier to talk to and get on with girls/women, just as they seem to find it easy to talk to and get on with me.

In High School, my closest friends were girls, my best friend was a girl, and not just because she had a beautiful older brother, I always got on with female teachers better than I did male ones too, with a few exceptions, of course.

I don't know if it's because I grew up around so many women, or because the women of my family and extended non-related family are of a similar outlook as I, perhaps it's because the women I know generally seem to be interested in why people behave the way they do, looking for answers and explanations of behaviour and attitudes, an interest we share. I am aware that I tend to get on better with men who are also interested in such things, so perhaps that is a factor in my relationships with people in general.

I also believe, in fact, I know, for myself at least, that different friends mean different things.

Everyone has a friend they can be absolutely entirely themselves with, and a friend they can call up when they want to go dancing or blow off some steam, or talk to about work, or about family issues or their ex. I am fortunate enough to have a group of brilliant friends, each with their own unique experiences, perspectives and sets of principles, each of whom I know I can talk to about anything, anytime.

Whatever the reason for our friendships, whatever the different links between us are, my girls have always meant the world to me, whether they are still in my life or not. They will always have a very special place in my heart as the girls who took the time to be my friends, the girls with whom I have shared so many of my life's wonderful and less-than wonderful experiences, the girls with whom I have always been able to be entirely myself.

So, here is a collection of some of the events and memories of my relationships with just a small handful of those wonderful girls & women.

17 Pieces

Susan

I can't remember exactly when I met Susan, only that she was there at a time when I needed some serious comic relief and a reality check or two. She was the first person who told me how destructive she thought my friendship with Natalia was, or at least, had become. That is something I will always be thankful to her for.

It's a funny thing with Susan, in my mind she was always there throughout my life in High School, especially in French & English lessons, but I don't think that happened until our first GCSE year, I guess that is the power of her personality! If I was the comedian, the one who mocked and got the laughs, she was the one throwing me the lines and bits of information to use, and she was also the one who laughed loudest and most often.

There is one specific memory I have of her that I will always cherish...

The Fields of Edgware

Summer, 1999

We had all just finished our last GCSE exams, and boy could you tell! Everyone was giddy with excitement and relief, at that point I don't think any of us really cared how we did in the exams, we were just glad they were over.

A group of us, what would eventually seem to be most of our year group, had decided that we'd all meet at our favourite Edgware pub for an evening of drinks and dancing. It was the height of summer, and today was a particularly hot day. We all donned our summer finest, I was wearing my favourite shirt, a blue Ben Sherman that I wore all the time, and headed to the pub.

It was one of those nights you see in films, where everyone just has a really good time, gets along, make several toasts and down several shots, dancing until they can dance no more.

The best part of the evening for me though, was at the end of the night, when, upon leaving the pub, all of us still chatting and laughing, I suddenly heard my name being roared in a faux-Irish accent (something we often did to each other), and having turned to look in her direction, saw Susan standing, shoes in hand, waiting.

Laughing, I asked what she was doing. "By a lonely..." she began to sing, and straightaway we launched into 'The Fields of Athenry' (a fantastic Irish folk ballad by Pete St. John), soon enough, she was jigging along to it too, there in the street in the summer's darkness. So, I kicked off my shoes and joined her. We jigged and sang, falling into each other laughing, enjoying being together.

It was one of those times where your stomach physically hurts from laughing so much, where you can't catch your breath, but don't want to stop. That was Susan.

17 Pieces

Eleanor

Eleanor was my comrade-in-arms during GCSE Maths. I think that's probably where our friendship started.

We were sat in the same row, with the central aisle dividing us, but were close enough to be able to whisper or pass notes to each other, which we frequently did.

Our teacher was off on maternity leave, replaced by a husk of a humorless human. On the rare occasion that she interacted with us, she spent more time talking at the whiteboard than she did looking at us, she would speak in a kind of vacant tone, in an entirely uninterested manner. This, of course, gave rise to our opting out of classes, not that we would bunk off school, we would go into class, but would spend the session, 70 minutes of maths, talking about things we'd done and seen at the weekend, things we were planning on doing that week, the latest film news, and whatever else we were interested in.

We would spend lesson after lesson talking about that week's episode of The X-Files, the story arcs, the mythology, David Duchovny - one of my first male crushes!

Out of those lessons grew our friendship, and when my GCSE Art teacher, who I adored (another woman, incidentally), left at the end of my first year of Art, I would start my Art classes then take a break under the guise of going in search of 'materials', but actually going to the Drama Studio up the corridor to see Eleanor and watch her group's latest rehearsal. Because of that, because of my friendship with Eleanor and the confluence of events that happened at that time, I saw and experienced a new kind of Drama lesson, one where the students played a more prominent role in devising their scripts, roles, and performances. That in turn would make Theatre Studies my Number 2 choice come A-Level selection (nothing could move English Language & Literature from the Number 1 spot!) and that selection would later result in a lot of positive personal changes for me.

We started A-Level Theatre Studies in the September, and were told we'd be performing a lengthy, character-rich play in the October. A slight panic rushed over me, this was a play with many scenes, and many characters, meaning we would each have to play more than one character. But, there was Eleanor, confident and enthusiastic, encouraging us all, keeping us going when we messed up our lines or staging, making us laugh with various impressions when we were tired from the previous night's late-running rehearsals. What could have been a nightmarish chore-like experience, was instead a lot of fun, thanks largely to Eleanor.

As time went on, and my confidence as a performer grew, so did my friendship with Eleanor. She soon became the person I sought out during free ('study') periods, or looked for when I wanted a cigarette between lessons, and she was always there, ready for a chat or a laugh, often with a new impression, accent or character to try out.

Shortly after I got with my first boyfriend, I decided it was time to tell Eleanor that I was gay. It was the first time I was ever going to admit it to someone, and I knew that she was the person I wanted to tell first. We were walking through the estate, at the end of which lay our High School & Sixth Form College, we'd been rehearsing our lines for a Theatre Studies performance, I think it was our mock exams, when I decided that now was the time to tell her. Upon hearing the words "Eleanor, I'm gay" she looked at me and said: "And...?"

That one word meant so much to me. With that singular word, she had said so much. She had let me know that my being gay changed nothing, wasn't anything particularly special, it was just what was normal for me. Just the act of telling her was enough, but her reaction was even better, and so entirely in keeping with her personality.

She became the only person I'd turn to when talking about my soon-to-be-ex boyfriend, asking what she thought about something he'd said or done. She was also the only person who truly knew where the filthy, purple lovebite I had on my neck was from, to which she again brilliantly and in another of her fantastic characters said:

> "Dutty tramp. For why you letz da
> boy suck on your neck like dat, bruv?!"

That was her way, it still is in fact. To put people entirely at ease in a seemingly effortless way.

She remains, though I don't see her anywhere near as often as I'd like to, one of the greatest friends I've ever had.

...she was also one of the girl friends who took me to my first ever Pride event. London Pride 2007, the day before I came out to Ma Newby.

Dean Newby

Lucy

Lucy will tell you that when she first started working with me over 10 years ago, I was the only person who spoke to her. It's certainly true that I made an effort to talk to her, to learn more about her, partly because I'm interested in people ("nosey fucker" she'd say), and partly because there was something about her that I instantly took a liking to.

The thing about Lucy is that she doesn't care what you think about her, if you don't like it you can "do one", it's not her problem.

Another thing about Lucy, is that beneath that tough, hilarious exterior, is a very kind heart, the heart of someone who looks after those she cares about. Though that isn't something everyone gets to see.

Yet another thing about Lucy, is that she is one of the few people I know who can equal and sometimes better me, when it comes to near-the-knuckle humour. We both walk straight up to the 'Line of Decency', that imaginary line that few dare to cross in the name of humour. Well, that line is where our humour begins, not leads up to. But, the decency we so like to make a mockery of is the old-fashioned, Victorian-values based decency, the sort that really isn't that relatable anymore. Of course, with an audience we go the extra mile to ensure that we make them, and each other, laugh.

That is where 'Lunches with Lucy' came from, we try to make sure that we are on the same lunch break, so we can chat and laugh, and make whoever else is on lunch with us, laugh too - though that's only the secondary objective, the primary being to make each other laugh. One of the skills we both quickly started using, was the art of the voice throwing, not in the way that ventriloquists do, but in a way that ensures only certain people can hear us - this is something I've been able to do for years, I don't really know how, it just seems to be something I can naturally do, and it is a tool that has come in very handy. There have been times that only Lucy has heard what I have said, as intended, and other times when a subset of those around us, those who have a similar sense of humour to us, have heard what we are saying, again, as intended.

Those 'Lunches with Lucy' have at times been the only thing that got me and, I think, her, through an exceptionally tough day at work, long may they continue.

Flo

Flo and I met 10 years ago while I was working as an IT Outreach Technician for a local college. She was a teacher in one of the 10 schools I visited every week, more than that she was a teacher in the school I visited on Friday afternoons, she was a fellow smoker (I have since quit), and friend to my brilliant on-site boss, the ICT co-ordinator - also a smoker.

So, after doing about half an hours work, which would coincide with her break, my boss would come and get me for a quick cigarette and catch up - she called them our 'Weekly Briefings'.

Dean Newby

The briefing generally took about a minute, it was a pretty easy school IT support wise, and I always managed to get a lot more work done in the 3 hours I was there, than any other IT technician they'd ever had - something I've always been proud of, my work ethic. The three of us would then spend the remaining one and a half cigarettes talking about things we'd heard in the Borough, ranting about the way Early Years was being treated by the government, and life in general.

I realised then that I'd met a kindred spirit in the form of Flo.

The way she spoke about Early Years, the passion, the dedication, her fierce defence of child-centered play and learning from experience, was almost exactly the same way that I spoke and continue to speak about Early Years.

She was a breath of fresh air.

I left that job after 20 months, finding my service-based, college boss too difficult to deal with anymore - she was a nice person, but didn't have a clue about how to talk to or interact with people, she was a by the book boss, we only did those things stipulated in the contract, which I understand is necessary for legal and accountability reasons, but if I see an IT problem (or, in fact, any kind of problem) and I'm able to fix it or suggest a way of fixing, I'm going to do just that. I consider it unprofessional and unhelpful not to.

Anyway, I digress...

So, I left that job, set up my own business and started working for my first client (the day after I finished working for the college). I can't remember exactly when Flo joined me at the school, it was a few years later, but there she was, full of life and energy, that passion not even the slightest bit diminished by time. We immediately picked up where we left off, becoming more friends than colleagues, made all the more better, when she was (eventually) named as the ICT Co-ordinator, and as such, my boss.

Our friendship made both of our jobs easier, we each knew what direction the other thought ICT should take (and we agreed entirely on that), we each knew the skills and talents of the other and had no issue deferring to the other when needed, and we both respected each other for the experience we each brought to the team.

Above all else, we were also both able to be direct about things that needed to be done, changes that needed to be made, all in the name of improving ICT in the school, and improve it, we did.

We made for an impressive team, ICT standards in teaching and pupil usage improved, people from the Borough were coming in to talk to us about the provision of ICT in both Early Years and SEN settings, and we were being awarded bid after bid for new ICT hardware and software. All largely due to our shared passion for education.

One of the defining moments of our friendship though, came when we discovered that we each had an immense love and admiration for The Killers, and of course, the beautiful man that is their lead, Brandon Flowers. Never before had I met someone who felt as strongly about The Killers and their outstanding music as I did, and soon we were comparing lists of favourite songs, albums, best lyrics, all the stuff that the superfans (that we are) do!

Then came my time to leave the school. I went unwillingly, but ensured I stayed in touch with Flo (and Patricia & Georgina), and a few months later Flo and I were dancing in the pouring rain of Hyde Park while The Killers blasted out tune after awesome tune on stage.

Fast forward a year, and we're back working together in a different school, she would claim that I followed her this time - which I guess I did, but only by a few months!

Her light still burns brightly, indeed, it seems to be burning brighter than ever, as does her love for The Killers - who we saw at Wembley just a few months ago.

Patricia

Patricia and I met while working at the same school in which I would later re-meet Flo, and later still meet Georgina.

As she tells it, I was: "a sweet, young chav" who she knew was gay from the moment she met me, but didn't tell me that until I came out about 18 months after we met. It wasn't really until that point, my coming out, that she & I became friends. We would have brief chats in her classroom, but the impact my coming out had on my confidence, meant that I was much more open with people and to the possibility of new friendships. Patricia was one of those who I made a concerted effort to get to know, and it actually proved effortless.

One of the things that we quickly found common ground over was a mutual disliking for another member of staff. This woman, Siobhan, was awful. She treated some people disgracefully, shouting at them in the corridor, telling them that they were wrong without anything to back up her judgement. To others, those that she liked, she was sickly-sweet, all over you, to the point where you would have to question her sincerity. That sincerity would be further questioned when it came to light that she had, in fact, been lovely to someone and then slagged them off behind their back in the staff room.

She was generally nice to me, but I was all too aware that she had also slagged me off before, and eventually played a part in my losing that school as a client. She also had big issues with Patricia, issues that she often found hard to quantify, because, as we were all aware, the real issue was that Patricia was a better teacher than her. She was a threat. But, in the larger, grander scheme of things, Siobhan was really quite inconsequential. Patricia & I moved on both physically and emotionally - Siobhan, however, is still stuck in the same place with the same feelings, and probably another victim in her sights.

A memory of Patricia that I love, probably because it was in the heyday of good times at that school, is of us; me, Patricia, Georgina, and another friend of ours, all having lunch in Patricia's class room - this was one of those things that started off as an unplanned event, soon becoming a regular feature of our working day.

Patricia had signed up to a dating website, and wanted our opinion on some of the men who she'd had contact with. We put the website up on the interactive whiteboard, and all sat like a panel of judges on some reality TV show. She started to go through the men, one by one, and we gave our verdicts on things they'd said in their profile blurbs, their pictures, stats, nothing was off limits - those poor men.

There were laughs at some of the 'Hey there...' approaches, sounds of 'Aww' at those who clearly had very little self-esteem, and a lot of 'What the fuck?!' to those who clearly had far too much self-esteem!

Having found not a single suitable person for her, I stepped up to the board and loaded the main screen. We then began sorting the general population into categories of: 'Hell Yeah', 'Yeah', 'Maybe', 'No', and 'Fuck No' - sadly, the 'Fuck No' category vastly outnumbered all of the other categories combined, but who ever said dating was easy?!

Now, when I say 'we' began sorting them into categories, I should probably point out that I had the final word on their categorisation. It came as no surprise then, that, upon looking at the 'Hell Yeah' category, a considerable number of them had beards/stubble and/or were either Italian/Spanish/Jewish. Not really Patricia's type...

When I turned around from the white board, having pointed this out, all of the girls burst into fits of laughter at my subconscious self-absorption. There was little else I could do but laugh with them.

There are two other things everyone should know about Patricia, that she would be furious about were they left out:

1. She is a 'gay man in a woman's body' - a phrase I used to describe her years ago, and something she is very proud of. Simply put, she talks about men the same way I and my gay friends do, she checks them out - sometimes quite obviously when we're out (I and so many of my gay friends do that too), and she has no issue talking about sex, again, something I and my gay friends do, regularly.

2. Her brother and cousin are two of the hottest men I have ever seen, so much so that I'm no longer allowed to talk about them, for fear that I'll get far too overexcited and give myself a nosebleed (that line came from another friend of ours!)

Deanna

I met Deanna years and years ago when she was dating a boy I was in school with. She always seemed nice, sweet, friendly. But it wasn't until I started getting back in touch with old school friends in 2007 that she and I properly spent time together.

Dean Newby

We quickly formed a strong bond, the sort of bond that is incredibly difficult to define.

It is just there, ever present, she gets me, and I get her, I can't tell you when that bond was formed because I honestly can't remember, it feels like it has always been there, or at least there from the moment we re-met in 2007.

I mean, obviously there are events that helped cement that bond; my misfortunes with men, Mexican-themed party nights, birthday parties of cowboy costumes, ginger cake, and a bodyguard-like-me, my misfortunes with men, London days and street food by the Thames, Thanksgiving evenings and getting lost on the roads of Harlesden, Half Term Hampstead fun, and so many others...did I mention my misfortunes with men?!

A love of good red wine, especially Rioja is also one of those things that the two of us have in common, it often playing a part in those events and memories. I always make sure I have a bottle with her name on it on standby, just in case she decides to pop over to see me.

But, there is one thing, one characteristic that we share that has always played a huge part in our friendship; our honesty with each other, our confidence in our friendship, to be able to tell the other when we think they're dealing with something in an odd way or are wrong about something - it very rarely happens, but the ability to do so is definitely there, as is our ability to make the other see things from a different perspective.

17 Pieces

Once, following a home cooked lunch at mine, during which Deanna and I discussed my then-current situation with a man and men in general, also known as my great misfortunes in the field of love and relationships (in fact, not even love, just the simple act of dating has all too often eluded me), Deanna came out with one of those wonderfully succinct and honest lines that only good friends can (and can get away with)

She, having sat patiently, listening as I rambled on about men, asked why I thought it was that I had such bad luck with them - she would also go on to reframe the argument, and suggest that I'd had pretty much the same amount of bad luck as anyone else, relatively. I gave her a list of factors, characteristics, expectations - from both perspectives; how I behave and expect them to behave, that sort of thing.

She sat and listened intently as I delivered an exceptionally long, unrehearsed and unedited list. Then, when I'd finished, she looked at me and said:

"You are Rain Man Newby! You're so focused on everything being in a precise, pre-decided way, that if it isn't, you get freaked out, and don't, can't just enjoy the moment! Ha, Rain Man Newby!"

We both laughed at my new nickname and her undeniably brilliant summing up of the situation. I wanted so much to have what so many of my friends had, at a time when my heart was still in its post-Zack ache, that I was being ridiculous when it came to my expectations, and as such, as she had stated, wasn't allowing myself to just enjoy the moment. This has thankfully now, many months later, changed - thanks largely to friends like Deanna.

She is one of those friends who I can talk to about absolutely and literally anything, never having to worry about if she'll judge me or my actions, always aware that the advice and support she offers comes from a place of true friendship and love for me, and us. I'd say that's the definition of a true friend, a best friend, which is why I am her GBF (Gay Best Friend) and she is my SBF (Straight Best Friend)

...she is also an 'Honorary Gay', a title given for her services to the gay community, namely, me.

Georgina

Everyone needs a Georgina in their life.

She is a bubbly, energetic force of nature, who can take you from 0 to 60 in under a second. Her effervescent, glowing love of life is too strong for even the saddest, angriest, loneliest person to resist. There is no choice, you are going to be happy too.

The list of reasons that I love Georgina is seemingly endless. But the core of it, the core of her is that which I've already explained above. She is a pure force for good in this world. She loves openly, always giving more than she receives. If you're excited about something, she'll be excited about it. If you're upset about something, she will sit with you (in kitchen, park, or pub) and talk you through whatever is going on in your life. She never has too little time for her friends.

She also has a Class A memory when it comes to other people's lives, as she so competently displayed a few years ago while we and some of my other friends were celebrating my birthday in the King William IV pub in Hampstead. One of the presents she and Patricia had bought me, was a sketchpad and felt tips, the sole purpose of which was for me to finally draw a diagram showing the links between my friends and social groups, and the people I've slept with.

We all set about drawing our own diagrams of my sex & social life. Mine got very messy, very quickly - I may publish it one day, with different names, obviously.

Others had drawn Venn diagrams, my name with sets of numbers linked to it, and all manner of other interpretations. As the time ran out, Georgina let out a scream of "Nooooo. Awwwwww", and showed us that she and Patricia, who were working together, hadn't finished yet.

What happened next was the truly brilliant part. As I made my way around the table, getting people to show and explain their diagrams, Georgina pointed out errors in the links, or people they had missed or placed too much/little emphasis on. The only diagram that came close to her knowledge of the subject, was mine, and even then she had some issues with it.

Dean Newby

That is Georgina. She is so interested in and committed to her friends that she remembers everything about them. Everything.

...she is also the person I celebrated the 2012 Olympic Games with in Hyde Park and beyond (she played a huge part in making the Olympics such a big deal for me), as well as one of the people I went to see The Killers at Wembley with, and the sole person (until she made friends with those standing nearby) that I saw Mumford & Sons at the Queen Elizabeth Olympic Park with.

...and, in return for a home-cooked dinner or out-and-about lunch, she is teaching me how to play the piano.

Simply put, she is amazing.

12 / 17
EQUALS WITH A SIDE OF PORK

Interviewer: In your first book, you talk a lot about your belief that every person you meet has some impact on your life, whether they are in it for a short or long period, can you expand on that?

Paul: Yes, as I say in the book if we are open to involving people in our lives, to allowing them to touch our lives, then we can truly grow as people - I see it as this: if you read one book your entire life, you will know that one story very well, but only that one story, only the characters and themes of that one story. If you read many books in your life, you will know those many books, all of their many, many characters and themes. Life is a library of people, how many books/people you read/know is up to you.

Interviewer: Interesting. So, what about those books that

aren't considered literary greats? Those people who don't really offer anything positive to your life?

Paul: There will always be people who only see the negative, the detractors, the critics, the 'enemies', but from that negativity you can glean some sort of lesson, though it may only be a minor one. However, you have to be ready for some serious soul searching, to answer some of the tougher questions about yourself, and to be entirely honest about the situation you found yourself in. It's not easy, but it's necessary.

Interviewer: But, what do you do about the person who is having the negative impact?

Paul: That's one of the toughest parts of it. If you decide someone is having a negative influence on your life, you can either talk to them about it in the hope that you can come to a resolution, or if it is beyond that, you have to remove them from your life as best you can - it can be hard, especially since they may be someone you have deep feelings about, or may be part of a pre-existing friendship group. But, you have to remove them. There is a reason that Doctors remove infected, dying limbs, don't underestimate the psychological threat of a constant nay-saying critic.

Interviewer: Ok let's move on to the happier and more positive side of relationships and people. You cite many examples of people who, from an early age, had a significant positive impact on your life. Do you think that's the case for most people?

Paul: I hope so. As children, we need and deserve as much love, affection, and encouragement as possible. We need people who can set boundaries, but can do so in a positive way, and can also appreciate that sometimes those boundaries can't be set in stone. I know that I grew up to be the person I am today because of the positive relationships I had as a child, with all manner of people from various backgrounds, ethnicities, and ages.

Interviewer: Wouldn't you agree though, that you were in a unique situation, considering your Mother's workplace was like a second home to you? And by extension, that her colleagues were like a second family to you?

Paul: I would agree with that, but I would add that so large is the impact and influence that they have had on my life and personality, that they are, in fact, part of my first family. I was immensely fortunate to grow up surrounded by loving, caring, open, intelligent people, not just in my blood relatives, but in my Ma's colleagues. Some of the biggest influencers of my life are from that place. I remember as a child, having a sort of epiphany or realisation that, these people who weren't related to me, treated me as one of their own, and cared for me in that same way.

Interviewer: So, of those seemingly wonderful people, is there one who particularly stands out?

Paul: Gabriella. Definitely Gabriella.

Interviewer: Why her?

Paul: Well, it isn't just that she stands out, it's that she was the first person, outside of the family, to treat me like an individual, not just a child or one of a group of children.

I don't remember the first time it happened, but I do remember being aware of it. It's like that for a lot of firsts I guess. Her name was Gabriella, she was a Portuguese Nursery Nurse, and the first person, outside of the family, to include me in an adult conversation, and to make me feel like an equal in a world of adults. I was around 10 at the time.

She was one of those people who had a glowing friendly face, a face that immediately put you at ease, soft and gentle, kind and warm, with a wisdom greater than her years, years that weren't shown with lines or crevices, but through tolerance and acceptance. She'd been through a lot in her life, I remember being aware of that quite early on, and you could be entirely yourself with her, in fact it was difficult not to be.

Interviewer: Is there a specific story or event when you realised she was treating you as more than a child?

Paul: Well, I'd realised some time before this event, but this is the main memory I have of that feeling, that realisation. Ma and I had gone to Gabriella's for dinner after work, she lived in a beautiful flat in Swiss Cottage, the sort of place you'd see in a glossy magazine. That was Gabriella, not in any sort of pretentious way, but just sheer elegance, a homely elegance of olive wood bowls and salad tongs, chaise long, hand stitched blankets, and fresh flowers - and this was before every TV show was about interior design, so she was in one sense a trend setter, and in another sense, the essence of Gabriella is that she really wouldn't have cared about that at all.

Anyway, I digress, we had eaten a gorgeous meal of new

potatoes and loin of pork in lemon & oregano, still one of my favourite summer dinners, and were sitting at her kitchen island, the only lights being the soft spotlights above and some even softer side lighting, it was quite late, but we were deep in conversation. We were talking about my Ma & Dad's recent breakup, and instead of asking the standard questions or expressing the usual condolences or platitudes, which though those asking didn't intend for them to be, always felt a little empty and rehearsed, Gabriella asked what I thought about it, how I felt about it, what I thought about seeing my Dad. That was something only a handful of people had done, all of them family or friends from school, none of them unrelated adults.

That was the moment that I realised Gabriella saw me as more than just a child, it may sound odd since all she did was ask me some questions, but by asking me for my thoughts and feelings on that and many other subjects, and somehow and with little effort creating an environment in which I could answer openly and honestly, she showed herself as a friend, as someone who cared for me. That is, after all what a friend is, someone you can talk to without fear of judgement.

Interviewer: She sounds like a very special person. Where is she now?

Paul: I don't actually know, she moved away many years ago now, and we lost touch. That happens too often, we lose touch too easily with those we shouldn't. But, as I mentioned earlier, I believe that people are in your life for various amounts of time, each of them having some sort of impact. Gabriella was there, in my life for quite a few years, and every day of those years it was an honour and a privilege to know her.

Shortly before she left, she told me something that I have always held dear, something that when I say it sounds immensely arrogant, but is, as far as she was concerned anyway, the truth. She told me that I could do whatever I put my mind to, and that I had a gift; a way of seeing things differently, of being able to communicate with anyone about anything. Now, I don't know if that's the case, I certainly hope it is, as a writer at least. I am aware though that it's something a lot of people say and have said to others, but there was something in the way she said it and again the fact that she was this unrelated, non-family person, that made me really believe her. That was the point that I really started thinking about my purpose in life, why I was here, and what I could and wanted to achieve.

Her belief in me, as well as the belief and support of so

many others, has been one of the key factors in my pursuit of my dream of becoming a published writer, in the hope that what I share through my writing may help someone or make them think about a situation in a different way.

Interviewer: You clearly believe in taking lessons from experiences, what lessons did Gabriella teach you? What lessons do you believe you taught her?

Paul: In all honesty, I don't know if I taught her anything, she was already wise before I met her. But, I'd like to think that though I may not have taught her anything, I made her happy, I know I was always able to make her smile, perhaps that's even better than teaching a lesson? There's not much point in learning if you can't smile.

On what Gabriella taught me, the lessons were vast. Most of them simply cemented already held beliefs - beliefs that stemmed from the teachings of my Ma, my grandparents, and others.

But, I would say that one lesson Gabriella taught me, in that impressively gentle unassuming way she could, was that expression of self, of thought, and tolerance for others, are themselves all independent of age, instead being based on a person's ability to communicate such beliefs and tolerance.

13 / 17
LOST LOVE, LOST US

Dear Lost,

In my 30 years on this planet, I've been fortunate enough to have many friends, people who I knew would watch my back, be there to catch me should I stumble and pick me up should I fall flat on my face.

Some have stayed a while then faded into the memory of school friendships and class room antics, others have stayed longer though the distance is wider than it once was - life is after all constantly moving, and sometimes we drift apart. Some have stayed the course, stitching the fabric of our friendship when its seams were fraying, making us stronger for it.

You don't really fall into any one of those categories...

We created a hell of a lot of memories together, summer gigs and dancing in the rain, house and dinner parties, trips to 'The North', holidays, picnics, terrified Halloween evenings, and Thanksgivings. So many good memories, times of us, a little younger, a little less tired perhaps.

Our friendship was, and I use 'was' tentatively, always so easy, it needed no real effort from either of us, we just clicked, you got me, and I got you. We had the same humour, though mine is a little crueller than yours, similar taste in men - or at least similar taste in what we wanted from men and relationships; honesty, kindness, care. And, sadly, a similarly destructible heart, one that we perhaps give away too easily to those who really do not deserve it!

But, we had each other to help the healing, the time you broke down in the street because your heart had been stolen and flung across the ocean? Only my arms could comfort you, and I knew before you even spoke that your soul was screaming. The far too many times that my heart on sleeve approach to everything failed, and left me feeling desolate and questioning, you were the one I always turned to, and you were always there to help in your unique heartfelt way.

Perhaps the effortlessness of our relationship was also part of its undoing? By never needing to make an effort, when it came to the point where one of us had to, we were oblivious to it until it was too late. Is it too late?

I know that I also played a part in our distance. I wasn't there, I wasn't present enough, I withdrew to focus on other things without explanation, you deserved more than that, better than that. I have now explained that to those who have asked and to some who haven't, to others, no explanation has been required, simply that I am back, is enough.

There were many reasons for my distance, before the repeating reciprocity of both of us widening the gap between us. Foremost was the combination of my relationship with Zack ending at almost exactly the same time that my main business client ended my relationship with them, and suddenly and dramatically cut my pay and working week! I honestly, and perhaps stupidly, never thought either of those would end, so to lose them both at the same time was something neither my head nor my heart could fully or coherently cope with.

I may be entirely incorrect on this, but I don't think I am, but my relationship with Zack, before, during, and after, and the destructive ripples it caused, must have played some part in our distance. It seems to be the pebble that caused the ripples on our calm, peaceful friendship - and not just ours, but others too. For that, I am sorry, not for the actual relationship - you know me far too well to know that I don't do regret, and I certainly don't do it when it comes to love...as destructive as that love may have been. There are certain things I know in this world, and following my heart is one of them, wherever or to whomever it leads.

But, I am also certain of this. You pulled away without explanation, without a fight, without once attempting to resolve or at the very least explain why you were widening the space between us. I deserved at least an explanation, even a row or argument of spitting cruelty would have been better than the doubting, questioning uncertainty of those few months I allowed my mind to focus on it.

I grieved for our friendship, for the us that was once so strong and seemingly unbreakable, untouchable. As with all grief, I went through the stages, I was angry, I was in denial - the period when I tried to continue as if we hadn't been out of touch for months, eventually coming to that wonderful point in grief where acceptance is really all there is left. With acceptance comes a shifted perspective, one not devoid of emotion, but simply more rational, and in my mind - the mind of someone who knows all too well their own failings and flaws, whose biggest critic is themselves, the rationale was simply this:

We had a strong, vibrant, active, friendship.

The actions I took, though you may have disagreed with or disliked them, shouldn't have caused the rip they did - in friendship, you have to have each other's backs, you have to support in good times and in bad, while balancing that support with questioning and constructive criticism. It is no easy thing to achieve, but it is worth it.

We allowed that rip to form. I tried to fix it, you only tried to try.

So, our friendship clearly wasn't as balanced or equal as I once thought; indeed, I've come to realise that a lot of relationships aren't balanced, perhaps that's the nature of humanity, that one person will always care or at least try more than the other.

If that is the case, perhaps true love between family, friends and lovers is when both people care equally? Maybe that's a romanticised, idealised version of love, but I'm a romantic idealist, so I like it.

For me, friendship, other than what I've already mentioned, is traversing London to my postcodal opposite for a 30 minute catch up over coffee when that's all your friend can do at the moment, because it isn't about the time or place, it's about seeing them, being there, being present, in all weathers.

I should say, that though it may not sound like it, none of

this is meant to blame, as I stated earlier, we both played a part.

I'm simply saying that our friendship shouldn't have ended that way, it shouldn't have been able to 'end' that way.

Somehow, perhaps because of our bond, there is still a part of me that wants our friendship to find new life, maybe we can never go back to how we were, that's ok, but it feels very unfinished, perhaps because of the lack of argument or falling out. You more than most know how rare that is for me, that if I feel I have been unfairly treated, I (eventually) cut the person off, declaring them as dead to me, which while it sounds overly harsh, for me is simply a matter of one of my rules of life:

No negative influences.

But that's just it, you're not, you never have been a negative influence, your influence just disappeared. I hope that our love is not, as this letter suggests, lost, but rather misplaced, simply waiting for us to rediscover it.

So for now, I shall simply say this: to be continued...

Dx

Dean Newby

14 / 17
CHAIN REACTION

Life's choices are like a hand outstretched...at the end of each finger is another hand, and another, and so on. The decisions we make form a unique path, the path we walk through life, oftentimes you can look back and see how you got to where you presently are, unable to change the past, but hopefully able to stop yourself from repeating the same mistakes in the future. We must never forget the ripples our actions can cause, what we do, how we are and behave to one another, can have a long lasting influence and impact on those around us.

What follows is the retracing of decisions made, thoughts and discussions had, and the path I took in one friendship that once was but is now no more.

Where it all began...

Robert criticised my lifestyle, stating that I was having too much 'fun'

(for those who are wondering, I still don't believe there's such a thing!)

▼

I thought about dealing with it, friends should advise and support, offering constructive criticism, not simply negative criticism - that's what enemies and detractors are for.

Instead I decided to brush it off, but, as you'll see, the seed had been planted.

▼

Robert, having just eaten a meal I'd prepared, declared that it didn't have any flavour. He was attacked by the other guests - his boyfriend and friend, for the baseless statement and rudeness of its declaration.

Indignantly, I said "Oh really? I thought it was full of flavour"

I didn't deal with the actual issue of his rudeness

▼

At the same dinner party, Robert left without saying goodbye or thank you

Later that week, instead of telling him that his behaviour was extremely rude and hurtful, I made a subtle point about it by asking him if something had upset him...he blamed his boyfriend.

▼

At a BBQ (at my house), Robert told me I was recycling incorrectly, when I corrected him, he still insisted I was wrong. I wasn't.

This is the point where I should have had a discussion with him, not because of the subject matter, but because the examples above are just a tiny handful of the comments and attitudes I had flung at me during that period. On their own, they seem inconsequential, but as a group they were part of a pattern of unacceptable behaviour.

Instead, I chose to keep the party's peace, and ignored his comment.

▼

Then came the news that Robert had, while talking to a mutual friend, suggested that I and his boyfriend were becoming closer than he would have liked. He never said this directly to me, just as I had never said how much his criticisms hurt and angered me.

I didn't talk to him about it, partly because it would put our mutual friend in the middle, and partly because if it was a problem he should have said it to me (just as I should have told him about how I felt about his behaviour)

▼

Then we went on holiday together...

Dean Newby

I don't know if it's because of the close quarters nature of such holidays, because I was often in a lot of pain (I got sunburnt on the first day, it got worse from then on...), or some combination of the two...perhaps it was simply that I'd had enough of him, but I snapped, bizarrely, at everyone except him.

That was entirely unfair, I'm not sure I've ever been so gutted and ashamed by my own behaviour.

▼

This is the part where there's a whole load of retrospection...

Robert & Zack broke up.

Soon after, I mean very (too) soon after, Zack and I went for dinner...and, as they say, the rest is history.

▼

At my birthday, just a few days later, Robert spent most of the evening talking to Zack. Of course, that was his right, no one can forbid someone from talking to anyone else...as much as they may want to!

I, in a (retrospectively) jealous-guilt-drink-fueled frenzy behaved (entirely out of character) like an utter cock to friends who had made the effort to come and celebrate my birthday with me. I was feeling sorry for myself, hadn't yet told anyone, anyone, about what was happening between Zack & I, and wanted some attention. Thankfully, I have some pretty amazing friends who, realising there was something wrong, just looked after me and did all they could to ensure I had a good night.

▼

I then, instead of being the friend I would ordinarily be, and for reasons of now obvious self-serving bias (my relationship with Zack) - though, at the time, it wasn't entirely obvious to me (kidding or lying to myself is not something I'm usually very good at!), began seeing less and less of Robert, in fact it became rare for me to see or have any contact with him at all. This was aided though not related to his falling out with a friend of ours, and so there were fewer social circles for Robert & I to inhabit simultaneously.

On this point, there wasn't any actual decision, it happened quite naturally, with very little fight from either of us - perhaps he saw, on holiday, that Zack and I had become closer than he & I, and so gave up? Perhaps he felt betrayed by that closeness, I've no idea. But it, for all intents and purposes, ended there.

▼

Then, came the decision to tell one of my most trusted friends about Zack. I hadn't told anyone about it, and I needed someone to talk to. I also knew that he'd have my back but would advise and question - his approach is almost always the tough but fair approach. It works.

So, one Sunday at mine as I peeled potatoes at the sink, I told him - it was a perfect 'Kitchen Sink Moment' worthy of a Brian Friel play. I told him everything, he asked some questions, then delivered a line that I will always remember:

"You wear your heart on your sleeve, we all know that. So, if you're following your heart, and you're being true to yourself, that's all that matters. But, be careful! Robert won't feel that way!"

▼

I then told some of my other close friends. I don't generally keep such things from my friends, it's rare for people not to know how I'm feeling, especially if I'm seeing someone. So, this whole concept of having kept such a thing from friends was entirely alien to me. They all took it in their own way, none of them were particularly negative, expressing more concern about how Zack may be treating me, than anything else. Most of them were surprised, some of them weren't at all, including one who had seen Zack & I out one night and gave a look of recognition, but never mentioned it again, thankfully - I wasn't ready to talk about it at that point.

I had made an active decision not to tell our mutual friend, the one who was having his own problems with Robert, as I didn't want him to feel he was in the middle of something and so had to act in a different way towards Robert, or I.

▼

A few months passed, Zack & I finished, and I decided to tell my friend about it.

So, on St. Patrick's Day 2011, I told him everything...starting with the simple line: Zack & I had a thing a few months ago - met with stunned silence, some questions which resulted in this brilliant and typically observationally accurate line: "Oh, so that's why you were like that at your birthday...and every other time you were drunk!"

▼

A few days later, that same friend sent me a txt...and if you've read the Introduction to this book, you know what it said.

The rest really is history now, but how scary it is to think that so many things, behaviours, moments, people, and the way we react can have such a long-term impact. Of course, I know they can, but in writing it down in this format, almost cold and rational, you can see more clearly how things come to be.

Our core group of friends suffered because of my actions and inactions, and while I have made attempts to repair the cracks, which were mostly successfully repaired, some of them grew too wide to be fixed, especially when one side of the crack didn't want to be fixed.

▼

All those things somehow came together to help create this book. The first idea for it, the structure, the purpose, all of that came from those fateful few months in 2010.

Dean Newby

SPEAK, HEAR, DO

PIECES 13 - 15

Dean Newby

15 / 17
DEFENDERS OF THE FAITH

School Opening Ceremony - Dedication Address
by Paul Newby

We stand here today, together, to mark the reopening of our great school.

When I was first approached and asked to think about making this dedication address, I knew immediately what I was going to talk about, it is something that many of us have discussed before, and it is something that must be spoken about, and it must be spoken about now, in this moment.

The issue at hand is the condition of the Early Years Education System in our Country, and moreover the efforts of those who work in that Education System, in our School, to improve those conditions.

If Early Years Education had a Doomsday Clock, then at this point, it would probably be set to about one minute to Midnight.

Dean Newby

Our troops; the Teachers, Teaching Assistants, Nursery Nurses, Head Teachers and all others who enlisted to serve and help in any way they can, have all put up a truly valiant effort, oftentimes in the face of utter adversity from an enemy with such little knowledge and experience in education that it makes a farce of their department, of their government, and is not worthy of our children, our parents, or us.

Education is more than learning a set of numbers, words or facts by rote. It is more than regurgitating that which we've read in a book.

Education is about enabling. It is about helping people become more than a set of drones, whose only relevant features are the set of statistics their time in education produces.

Early Years Education, and beyond, is about giving people the tools and skills to not just read and learn the facts, but to be able to discuss them, to use them when arguing a point, to have a point of view in the first place, and most importantly to have the confidence to think for themselves and share their thoughts, even if those around them believe them to be incorrect.

Education is not about ensuring that all children can write their names by the time they're three years old, especially when they may have only entered nursery two weeks earlier!

Education is not about asking closed, single answer questions.

Education is about asking open multi-answer questions from which the person can and will, in a positive, open learning environment, talk about what they think, sharing both related and sometimes unrelated points.

Education is not about continual, lengthy assessment, especially when that assessment takes so much time that the educator gets very little face time with the children. Indeed, if educators aren't present because they're assessing that much and that often, what exactly can they be expected to assess?

Who has been there to teach those they are assessing that which is being assessed?

Who has been there to answer the questions of the naturally inquisitive, or encourage those who might not yet have the confidence to ask such questions.

We all know that assessment is important, it is how we know what next steps to take with each child, but it is equally important, if not more so, to allow and encourage each child to be a part of deciding which steps they want and need to take next, letting them be a part of their path of learning, putting them at the core of their education.

It is also about trusting that every good educator will pick up on, from their time with the children and from observations in the class room and beyond, the less obvious signs of learning, the smaller steps they have to take before they have all of the skills or knowledge to take the bigger ones.

Education is about the child, every individual who walks through our class room doors has to be treated as such, and should feel that the education they are receiving, that they are a part of, is specifically for them, designed around them, to help them become better, more independent learners.

Dean Newby

Education is about creating independent, self-motivated learners.

Learners who are not afraid to raise their hand and ask a question.

Learners who want, who need, to know the how, the who, the when, and the why.

Learners who can invent a game or activity that involves every one of their peers, and embraces that which they have learnt.

Thankfully, there are those among us who are putting up a good fight.

Who are refusing to change the way they teach and interact with children, who are putting their careers on the line by telling Ministers, Inspectors (some of whom have only taught for a fraction of the time that those they are inspecting have, and some of whom clearly do not understand the age range they are inspecting) and Local Authority hacks, that they have it wrong, that they have no idea what they're talking about, that the questions in their lip-service consultations are evidence of an absolute lack of understanding, care or respect for what makes a good Early Years education and educator.

These people, these dedicated, passionate, experienced people, our people, are standing firm for us and our children, they are standing firm because they know that the alternative will result in the cataclysmic collapse of our Early Years education system as we know it.

What we know of it, is that it is, or at least can be an outstanding education system, provided those who know nothing about it, haven't worked in it, or who don't really have the children's best interests at heart, back off and allow us to get on with the job, the job that we know, the job that we love, the job that we entered because we wanted to help make the world a better place.

A better world, is a place where everyone has access to a good education, where people are taught to think for themselves, to think beyond what they already know or have experienced, to question, to analyse, to evaluate.

To throw light upon the darkness of ignorance, that is one of the truest goals and best outcomes of a good education.

These brave, bold educators are standing firm because they want the word 'educated' to mean what it once did; being able to communicate ideas, beliefs and knowledge in an articulate and coherent manner.

They are standing firm because they do not want to see their classrooms become factories for the creation of identical automatons, filled with facts but lacking the skill to analyse or communicate those facts.

They are standing firm because they care about the future of our country, of our world, and they know that our children are that future, that we have a duty to prepare our children in the best way we can for that future!

They are standing and have been standing on their own for far too long.

Let us now join with them, shoulder to shoulder, resolute in our commitment to deliver an education of inquiring minds, where what we teach is based on the now, not just the then, the learner, not the assessor.

To finish, I would like to thank all those who have put up such a brave fight, who continue to fight for that which we know is right, who even when being beaten down by the system and its utter ineptitude, still keep fighting the good fight.

And so, I dedicate this school to all of them, to all of you, Our Educators, without whom I would not have been able to write this speech.

Our children, and our children's children are relying on us. Let us not fail them.

Thank you.

16 / 17
MUSIC SEEN

Music has the power to bring smiles of memories past, and tears of both joy and sadness. It can be a comfort, reminding us of times of happiness, people we love, and places we visited. It can, however, also be a curse, evoking memories of times of sadness and desperation, people we have lost, and places we'd rather never revisit.

So, just what is it about music that can do all of these things and more? Why do we form attachments to certain songs? Why do songs, that we may have heard a hundred times, remind us of that one moment in time, good or bad, happy or sad?

I think it depends on how much of a part music has played in your life, and possibly how early on that influence took hold. As with so many things in life, music is something that offers familiarity, that helps us establish our place in both our local social groupings, and the larger, ever changing world. It can also be that which enables us to interact with social groups, giving us something to talk about. Music like other art forms has its followers and fans, an instant social group within which we can discuss and enjoy a song, an album or the entire works of a singer or band.

But, music can also be a deeply individual thing. Some songs are meant just for you, for your own enjoyment - whichever emotion they may evoke. As such, some memories associated with music may be of a decision you made while listening to music, or simply the act of listening to the piece of music. Once, while in a particularly bad mood at work, a colleague and friend commented: "Ah, didn't you get your morning music?" at first I didn't know what they were talking about, then they explained that they had noticed I was more energetic and happy when I'd walked to work listening to my music - they were right, I am happier, more productive and more focused when I have or am listening to music. Oh, and also, they were correct about that morning, my MP3 player's battery had died about 10 minutes after I'd left the house!

Music has been a huge part of my life for as long as I can remember. Most of my earliest memories contain a song, sometimes simply as a backing track, other times as the main feature.

For instance, music playing on Saturday mornings while Ma cleaned the net curtains and windows, it was always either UB40, Crowded House, or The Housemartins, sometimes the wonderful Tracy Chapman or Rod Stewart, and it was always playing at full volume from the old Woolworths cassette player in the kitchen.

The memory of an aunt's birthday party. I don't remember anything else other than the fact that Kool & The Gang's 'Celebration' was playing - this was also a turning point in my thinking, because it was the first time I realised that music could be requested in public places - to a child, the idea of coincidence is a strange and unlikely thing - surely everything that happens around you, is either for or because of you?

Paul McCartney's 'We All Stand Together' (from 'Rupert and the Frog Song'), was the first piece of music I ever remember owning, it was a cassette tape, the case was red, and it was accompanied by the book of the story - the back of which had the sheet music for the song. I played that cassette nonstop, sitting in the kitchen, book in hand, listening, waiting. I'm also very much aware of the fact that the point of the song, what the frogs are singing about, standing together, never giving in, fighting the fight, is something that I strongly believe in, it is part of my core being. Did that sense of determination come from the song? Possibly. At the very least, it was something that evoked and still to this day evokes that same feeling.

I also couldn't write this piece without including two memories of music with my grandparents - they introduced me to the majority of the music I listen to today (either directly or through their influence on Ma), and their love of music is definitely something that has rubbed off on me.

The first such memory, is of my nan wrapping Christmas presents in the box room, surrounded by wrapping paper, ribbon and bows of every size and colour imaginable, while from the record player Jim Reeves sang 'Silver Bells'. The other is of my grandad listening to Bruce Springsteen (or Fleetwood Mac, Bryan Adams, Mike & The Mechanics, The Pet Shop Boys...to name but a few!) on full volume in the back room, while sitting just a few feet away from the speaker - you could literally hear the music from about halfway down the road, as I often did while walking home to theirs after school on a Friday.

Dean Newby

Then there are memories of live music, again from an early age. I remember Sunday afternoons at my nan & grandad's house, two of my uncles chatting and playing guitar in the box room upstairs. I would go and sit, quietly, watching them as they suggested various chords and songs to one another.

I've been extremely fortunate to, over the last few years, attend some absolutely amazing gigs. The most recent are also my two favourite gigs of all time, not only because they are my two favourite bands of all time, but because of the venues, the atmosphere, the entire experience. I would even go so far as to say they were as close to spiritual experiences as I think I've ever had.

On the soundtrack of my life, these two bands appear more times than any other band, group or soloist, they are: 'The Killers' and 'Mumford and Sons'. Putting aside my crushes on Brandon Flowers and Ben Lovett - both beautiful and so talented, the bands are lyrical geniuses, with catchy tunes, not just in that catchy 'pop' way either, brilliant musicianship and outstanding vocals. All of those factors make for bands that deserve so many places on my list.

I've seen The Killers live three times, each time somehow better than the previous, and each time discovering something new that I love about them or experienced during the gig. At their most recent gig, I was on hallowed ground, the (plastic-covered) pitch of Wembley Stadium. Wembley means many things to many people, primarily football fans, where the hopes and dreams of our nation lay upon the shoulders of the players of our national team, always looking to relive the glory that was '66. But for me, Wembley means watching the laser shows of gigs past from the balcony of my first home, a flat in a block of countless homes, called George Lansbury House in Harlesden. From that balcony, we could hear the music, and on still nights could even make out the lyrics, all while lasers pulsed through the night sky like signals to an orbiting ship. The famous Towers of Wembley could be seen from my Primary School, and the now famous Wembley Arch can be seen from my front room, so Wembley has always, in some small part, been part of my life, or at least existed on the outskirts, there in the corner of my eye.

I think it was a mix of Wembley's significance and The Killers' sheer skill, passion and energy that made that gig one of the most spiritual experiences I've ever had. We were all singing in unison, everyone jumping and arm-waving at the same time, silence falling when we came to a softer more intimate song, everyone there seemed to be feeling it too, especially when phones were taken out, and with light emanating from the screens, we swayed in time with the band and their song. The crowd erupted when the specially written 'Wembley Song' was performed, with people recognising the various parts being sung about - from football, other bands, and The Killers' big break in London all those years ago! Simply awesome in the truest meaning of the word, I was awe struck.

The Mumford and Sons gig was held at the Queen Elizabeth Olympic Park, home to the London 2012 Olympic Games, and the sporting hopes and dreams of our nation. 2012 was an incredible year for London and the rest of Great Britain, not only did we do incredibly well in the actual Olympic Games, but the show we put on, the entirety of what was London 2012 was so hugely and immensely impressive that I think it will probably be one of the greatest sights in living memory for at least the next generation or two. So, when Mumford and Sons came to perform their gig here, handpicking the acts that would perform before them, they had to deliver, and deliver they

did, in every sense. The atmosphere was electric, thanks in
part to the venue, it was hard not to relive the glory and
memories of 2012, but also in part due to their sheer
brilliance, reacting to the crowd and our support and love
of and for them, singing back every word, every line in
unison, as one again, as we were in the glory of 2012, all of
us fans, all of us there to see the band that we loved, whose
music meant so much to us. All of us jubilant, uplifted,
fans.

I also have a memory, not of live music itself, but of the
event that is live music. My uncle and his band were
performing at the Mean Fiddler in Harlesden, Ma & my dad
were going to watch him, my grandparents coming over to
look after me, and though I wasn't going myself, I
remember being excited by the idea of my uncle on-stage in
front of all those screaming fans - that's how I imagined it
anyway.

As well as memories being recalled at the sound of a song, I
also find myself imagining scenes. In fact, it is more
common for me to envision a scene when listening to
music than it is for me not to. I remember, as a child,
thinking that this was normal, that everyone did it - I was
aware that they may think or imagine different things to me,
but I wasn't aware that they may not do it at all, until I
described a 'Music Seen' to a friend in Secondary School,
who shook his head the entire time, and asked: "Where did
you get that from?" I then spoke to my drama teacher about
it, who, being the fantastically enthusiastic art-embracing
person that she was (in the film of my life, she would be
played by the wonderful Emma Thompson), told me to
write them down, that they could form part of a story, or
that from one, a story could spring. So I did.

17 Pieces

Tintinnabulum, Karl Jenkins

A huge, sweeping city of old. The city is made of rock and stone, very natural, immersed in nature, surrounded by magnificent old trees as far as the eye can see. At the center of the city stands a huge set of steps, wide at the bottom narrowing towards the top.

Thousands of people are in the area near the base of the steps. Some are holding staffs atop which sit glowing orbs. They are waiting. A woman wearing a beautiful cream dress and headscarf of silk appears, accompanied by two men - one on either side. Her hands are clasped in front of her. She begins the walk up the steps, the two men always one step behind her.

As the three of them reach the top, which has a ring of dignitaries waiting, all of whom are clapping, the three all turn to face the crowds below, the two men still slightly behind the woman. The woman smiles at the crowd, her smile is caring and warm, compassionate. She feels responsible for them.

The woman throws her hands into the air, as she does, the two men do the same, all three sending a handful of petals high into the air - the petals are the colours of their city's flag. A huge roar of cheers and screams from the crowds below and behind.

The petals gently flutter on the warm breeze, floating down towards the crowd. The woman looks to the two men who now step forward and in line with her, she takes their hands, and together they raise their arms and smile. There has been a long, hard fought battle, but finally, they are victorious.

Dean Newby

Lover of the Light, Mumford & Sons
(Instrumental: 3:22-4:22)

I see a convoy of battered cars, trucks, racing through a dirt track, dust billowing up as they go, the rumbling sound of the vehicles combines to one sound or feeling of immense immediacy.

They need to get there, they need to get there now. The scene moves focus to a man, face covered in sweat and dirt from the road, from his journey before where he currently is. A look of absolute determination on his face, he stares glassy-eyed through the windscreen, he's thinking "I'm coming. Hold on. Just. Hold. On"

Angel in the Night, Basshunter

A gay night club full of men dancing, sweating, it is packed wall to wall, there are small platforms scattered around the dance floor, and a multi-level stage at one end of the room. A group of friends are dancing, they're all dressed in trousers and shirts, they're well-kept men. This song comes on, and the club goes wild for it, everyone is dancing in perfect time, emphasising the particularly electro-dance bits with hard deliberate angles.

On the stage, a man suddenly appears, he is looking at one of the men in the group, the light haired one. He in turn notices the man on stage, and soon realises that he is singing to him.

With each word that he sings, the man on stage mimes a corresponding action, but he is no longer simply on stage, he is calmly making his way towards the single member of his audience at whom his performance is aimed. The light haired man, still with his friends, can't quite make out who this singing man is, but he is familiar.

Now, his group of friends realise that he isn't dancing entirely in time with them, and as they look at him they see that he is staring at something beyond their group. They turn, and upon seeing the singing-dancing man, a look of recognition covers each of their faces.

The singing-dancing man now steps onto the platform the group is dancing on, as he does this, the rest of the group step off to give him and their friend room. Now their friend, the light haired man finally realises who it is. It's his friend, the friend he has always felt something for, something more than friendship, he hasn't ever felt anything like the connection he feels when he's with him, and now, that connection feels even stronger, and it's written across both of their faces.

As they step closer together, the song ends, and as the singer-dancer lowers his hands from his final dance-move-hand-action, his light haired friend, Ben, who he has loved since the first time they met, takes his hands in his own, their fingers interlock, and they step even closer together, and gently they kiss for the very first time. Around them, their friends can be seen smiling in delight that they have both finally acted upon their feelings.

Without You, Harry Nilsson

The entire scene is in sepia. A young girl in her early 20's, with long soft brown hair, wearing a tweed jacket, is standing by her bedroom door on the landing of her house. She is holding a small brown leather suitcase, it has some stickers on it, they are of places she has been - Paris, Rome...others. She is leaving, again.

Dean Newby

She quietly closes the door, and carefully she creeps down the stairs, making sure not to step on the creaking part of one of the steps. She rounds the corner, and through the open living room door, she can see the light of the television flickering on the smoke stained flock wallpaper, the sound of him snoring just audible over the television's sound. Wednesday night television programming, so dull.

She carefully tiptoes backwards towards the front door, and picking up her umbrella, she reaches for and turns the door handle. It clicks open, and in one swift movement, she slides out through a gap just big enough for her and her case. She closes the door firmly behind her, and hurriedly makes her way down the broken slabs that were once the path to their happy home.

She passes under a street lamp, her shadow streams across the street. She crosses, takes a left around the corner and is gone.

Give Me A Little More Time, Gabrielle

A teenage boy and girl sit on a red brick wall, the boy is smoking. They are talking about their friends, their family, having one of those catch ups that close friends have. They each make the other laugh without any effort, they both understand what the other is saying even when they can't find the necessary words. The girl is talking about her boyfriend, her friend sits listening, looking at the floor as he inhales, the ash on the end of his cigarette hasn't been flicked off since he started this one, it's now almost half the length of the cigarette itself.

He soon realises that he has zoned out because he can hear that his friend has had to repeat herself. "Well, what do you think? What should I do about it? Should I do it?" He looks at her, really looks at her, she notices and moves her head so that it is at the same angle as his. Her eyes are concerned, questioning. Her mouth is half open, waiting to respond to whatever advice he gives her about her current predicament.

He shifts his gaze from her eyes to her mouth, then back up to her eyes and says: "I'm in love with you"

They both freeze, their lives paused for a moment, just a moment. This moment.

I Wish I Never Met You, Sam Sparro

A London street, it's night time. The road and pavements are wet, spots of rain can occasionally be seen through the light of the street lamps. A couple are arguing, one is wearing a denim jacket, sleeve cuffs turned up. His hair is a mess from the rain and from running his hands through it to calm himself down so that he can think. He has been crying.

His boyfriend, slightly taller, with dirty blond hair, and a ring piercing in the top of his left ear, is trying to reason with him. Pulling on his arm to get hm to slow down, come back to him, and talk about it. The smaller one is having none of it and is getting more and more agitated.

Now, as dawn is breaking, and the London sky is a mix of blue and white clouds, the pair stand by a doorway, silent. The taller one has his leg propped up behind him against the door, hands in pockets, he is pale. The other one has bloodshot eyes and looks exhausted. Taxis pass, the hum of city life begins to grow louder.

The taller one steps away from the door and says: "That's

that then. I'm done." and walks away passing the smaller one as he does. They don't look at each other. The smaller one stays, staring up at the sky.

Flume, Bon Iver

A young couple drive along a hilly road in an old, faded, blue car, possibly a pickup. The man has brown wavy hair, the girl long blond hair with soft 'English-Rose' skin. As they drive, the hot summer sun beating in through the back window, a warm breeze streams through the half opened side windows, bringing calm and tranquility with it.

Their love is still new, they are entirely open to all the possibilities of the future, their future, but this is where they are right now, this is the only place they want to be right now.

The man looks at his love and smiles to himself, she sees this and looks directly at him, reciprocating the same smile. The sort of smile that only two people in love can share, the smile of them, of the possibilities, of being so entirely and all-encompassingly in love.

They keep driving.

Earlier, I mentioned the 'Soundtrack of my Life', this does actually exist, it is a playlist of songs that define various eras, events and moments of my life.

You can view and listen to the playlist via the 17 Pieces website at www.17pieces.co.uk

17 / 17
LONDON FOUND

On a few brilliant occasions when I was a young teen, I and my cousins went into town to meet my uncle for a film, dinner, or to spend time simply mooching around (though I'm not sure the word 'mooching' existed then?!) and looking at comics in local comic stores.

Those occasions were my first set of introductions to Central London, that place that as a child growing up in North West London, seemed like some far foreign unseen land, an unknown place of posh people, banks and politicians, the river, and a handful of tourist attractions. Of course, I was aware of its history, of the significance of things that had and were still happening, and of the cultural significance - plays and musicals, some long-running others short-lived.

But, I hadn't until then experienced any of that for myself, I was removed from it, not a part of it, therefore didn't have any form of emotional bond or attachment to it. That all soon changed.

Dean Newby

I still remember wandering around the streets of Seven Dials in utter awe of the buildings, of the beauty of it all, of the mix of people - and I'm from Brent, so a mix of people is nothing out of the ordinary to me, but this was different, this was more concentrated, this was tourist land. My uncle had a wonderful way of truly wandering, taking his time, no stress, and very few time restrictions, just focussing on those who were with him, taking the time to walk and talk, to stop whenever one of us wanted to look in some shop window - usually at either a comic or a gadget.

With every few steps, it seemed as if London was unfolding in front of my eyes, opening up and showing me what it had to offer, what I could be a part of if I just visited a little more often. Sadly, school work and exams soon became my main focus, and I had to forget about (Central) London for a while.

Skip ahead a few years, post-school, post-college, working-life-all-grown-up-ish, and my decision to finally come out to my family, which was an amazing experience. Shortly after my coming out, my uncle, the London Introducer, invited me to lunch at Balans on Old Compton Street, which I, even as someone who had never been, knew was the aorta of Soho. This would be my first trip into Soho proper. I remember being strangely nervous, not at all about seeing my Uncle, but about venturing into the uncharted territory of the Gay Village, such as it is. Still, I had just come out, was feeling immensely positive and confident, ready to take on the world...or at least, for now, have a lovely lunch with my lovely uncle!

I got lost.

Somehow between Leicester Square Station and Old Compton Street, a walk I can now do with my eyes closed or even while drunkenly stumbling, I took a wrong turn, then another, and another, continually refusing to give in and call my uncle for directions. So, I remained lost until he phoned me and after some merciless mocking (as he was right to do!), he gave me directions to the restaurant. In some bizarre way, all the distraction of being lost and late, made me forget entirely about my nerves of entering Soho, and I marched, maybe even strutted my way down Old Compton Street and into Balans, where I eyed up a waiter or two, ate the best ham and eggs ever cooked, went several rounds of mockery with my uncle, and discussed philosophy, humanity, the human condition, and our wonderfully unique family, and finally, I felt truly at home in Central London.

Shortly after that, I started campaigning with LGBT Labour for the 2008 London Mayoral Election.

We met in Soho one Friday evening, and I immediately felt like one of them (because I was, am!), it really was one of the friendliest, easygoing groups of people I've ever met, indeed some of them are now my closest friends, and there may have even been one or two there who would eventually become an 'ex'. We walked the streets handing out leaflets, discussing policy and signing up new members, and I felt like part of something, something important, something that was bigger than me.

I realised that when talking to people on Old Compton Street, I was using the fact that I was a Londoner to explain why they should vote for Ken (Livingstone). I was, without rehearsal, coming out with lines like "Don't you think our London deserves a Mayor who calls it 'Our London' too?" and "As someone from London, I honestly don't think anyone else has worked as hard, as long or as passionately for us - both people who live here and LGBT people, as

Dean Newby

Ken has. Do you?"

That was further confirmation that I was part of London's fabric, and that it was, indeed, part of mine.

Of course, that was also the night that I met Isaac...but that's a whole other story, and piece!

When people ask me where I'm from, I tell them I'm from London, but immediately and automatically follow that with "born and bred."

I haven't always done that, it seems to have begun around the same time as I started socialising more, expanding my social circles, meeting new people, campaigning with LGBT Labour. My declaration of "born and bred" is born out of meeting so many people who aren't from London. Literally most of those in my social and friendship groups aren't from London, though for many it has become their adopted home, loving it as much as I who was born here. Well, almost as much anyway.

There are friends from Plymouth, Cornwall, Manchester, Liverpool, and several places in between. Then the further afield, Canada, Australia, New Zealand...so very few from London. One of the few fellow Londoners is George. When I first met George, we were both pretty amazed to find that the other was from London, let alone that we were 'Borough Neighbours' - he Harrow, I Brent.

Something I quickly came to realise, through having all of these non-Londoner friends, was that most of them knew more about parts of London than I did. I was suffering from that strange affliction of not having to bother because I was from London, it was my home, so there wasn't any need to explore it like you would some European city or

17 Pieces

American state you were holidaying in.

So, I set about correcting that, asking my friends for advice on places to go, arranging day trips made up largely of wandering through old streets of The City of London and the East, the several parks that make up so much of our wonderful city, the markets bursting with fresh produce and Dishy Daddies, the fabulous museums, galleries, monuments and statues, not to mention more than a few pubs, bars, clubs and cafes along the way.

I soon became properly acquainted with My City, and I felt all the more better for it, for now I could truly call it mine. Along the way, I found places that have since become some of my favourite places in London, possibly the world. The places I go when I want to relax on a summer's afternoon, or write when it's cold and raining out, places where fun is always guaranteed, places of utter beauty, and cafes and restaurants with magnificent culinary delights! There are also a few places associated with memories, people, the people without which a lot of places would simply be devoid of all purpose.

On the following pages, I have listed and described 17 of my favourite London places and areas.

The 18th and last London place on my list is one that is gone, but will never be forgotten.

Dean Newby

*The Jubilee Line from Wembley Park to Stanmore
& the walk from Stanmore Hill to Brockhurst Corner*

This one is an entirely personal favourite. The train to Stanmore has, for me, long been filled with feelings of familiarity and happiness, it is the train that takes me to my nan & grandad's house, to weekends with the entire family, walks in the woods, football & base-making in the garden, Christmas dinners and teas, and everything in between. But, there is also something else I find special about the train ride, and it begins as you pull out of Wembley Park station (heading Northbound) - quite suddenly, the industrial, grey, warehouse & train-shed surroundings open up to a greener, leafier, more residential London.

The Kingsbury & Queensbury tube station platforms are smaller than those of the stations before them, and beyond the railings, trees and houses can be seen. Then onto Canons Park, where the platform is reminiscent of that from a 1940's black and white film - you can almost see the steam billowing along the platform as some leggy starlet in a grey jacket (with a brooch, of course) and hat wanders the platform looking for her love.

The short distance between Canons Park and Stanmore is lined with houses whose gardens seem, and probably are much, bigger than those south of here. More trees and grassland seem to poke out of every non-residential area until the train pulls into Stanmore, an old, but recently-updated village station with several steps to the top and street-level. Even the station's entrance reminds me of the sort of place you see at the seaside, immediately in front of you but across the road sits a long road-dividing island with all manner of greenery and beautiful flowers sprouting from it. This may just be me, but I'm sure the air here is clearer.

The walk from the station along the A410 (Uxbridge Road)

takes you through Stanmore Village, past the Pizza Express where many a birthday dinner has been had, past Bernays Memorial Hall and Bernays Gardens, onward past St John's Church, then the long stretch of the Uxbridge Road until you get to what used to be RAF Stanmore Park station but is now new-build houses and apartments. Forward a little more and you reach my nan & grandad's road, one of the widest residential roads I've ever seen, with pavement and grass on each side, ending where 'The Woods' (Heriot's Woods and Bentley Priory Nature Reserve) begins. It is amazing to think that just a short tube journey from Central & North-West London can take you to real woodlands, with trees that look like something from a Tolkien realm, and a still quietness that allows you to listen to and take in the nature that surrounds you.

The Edgware Road (and the bits between)

It's like the spinal column of my life skeleton, the central part off which so many other parts connect. Starting at Stanmore, home, as you've already read, to my nan & grandad, where my mum and her siblings grew up, where I and my cousins spent so many weekends playing in the garden. Then down to Edgware and Cafe Edge where I could be found singing 'The Fields of Athenry' (by Pete St. John) at chucking out time, down to Colindale where I went to High School and spent so much of my adolescence, walks with Natalia, had my first of many drinks in the cluster of pubs by Wakemans Hill Ave, and had my first kiss.

Onwards to Staples Corner, home of Chiquitos where many a fun night was and still is had with fellow colleagues and friends, flirting with the waiters (especially Rob), and getting more and more raucous. A little further on to Dollis Hill and where I now live, The Ceili House on the Hill, where I went home to Ma & my Stepdad when things got too tough, and now have brilliant parties, dinner and the occasional BBQ. On to Cricklewood and nights out at Ashtons and the Galtymore, visits to my paternal grandparents and being taught how to shoot (an airgun) and play poker, and weekends at Brendan's reading papers, watching films, all while usually recovering from the night before.

Then down the road to Kilburn and Sunday catchups over coffee with friends, Christmas shopping on the High Street, too many brilliant deals in Poundland, and birthdays, leaving do's and summer fun in the pubs that line the road. On through Maida Vale to Edgware Road Station and campaigning for the 2008 London Elections and 2010 General Election, leafleting the high rises and multitude of shops and restaurants - and where I first tasted and fell in love with Indian food.

Then to the end of the road at Marble Arch and into Central London, where so many memories and most of my favourite places are, not least of which is...

Hyde Park

An awesome park in its own right, but made more so by the number of brilliant festivals, gigs and events it has hosted over the years, especially recently! It was here that I first saw The Killers live at Hard Rock Calling 2009, and then again in 2011 (with James playing a brilliant set beforehand). I took my then boyfriend to Hard Rock Calling here in 2010, where we saw Crowded House & Paul McCartney perform brilliant sets, and later that week I saw the simply amazing P!nk at the Wireless Festival, and Barenaked Ladies & Rod Stewart at 2011's Hard Rock Calling!

But, it was also here that I experienced the 2012 Olympic Games, courtesy of BT London Live, and they put on quite a show...and a free show at that! Screens showed the live action from the Olympic Park and other venues, Team GB Olympians took to the stage and were met with cheering like I've never heard before, taking the time to answer questions - in between screams and further cheers from the crowd, then autographing, shaking hands and hi-fiving (I was delighted to get an autograph and hi-five from the adorable Peter Wilson - who won us a Gold for Shooting) and in between events and later in the evening, various bands and acts would take to the stage to entertain us - Cast, Amy MacDonald, Aiden Grimshaw, and the absolute brilliance of both The Overtones and The Noisettes, and all under the watchful, ever-helpful eye of the fantastic Team London Ambassadors, without whom it wouldn't have gone as well or smoothly.

We were all united in our delight at a job well done from the mesmerising, stirring Opening Ceremony, to the Golds won by so many of Team GB, and from that point on, everyone finally seemed to be talking so positively, proudly and passionately about London, about what we were and could accomplish if we all worked together, it was a truly moving thing. I don't think I've ever seen so many people welling up when watching TV as I did while watching the Closing Ceremony in a Soho bar, the tears weren't just because these weeks of sheer brilliance were coming to an end, they were tears of pride, of the realisation of just how great Our City is. That's probably the best thing to come out of the Olympics for me.

Dean Newby

The Heights at St Georges Hotel

Wonderful for a post-work cocktail, or three, with friends. It has amazing views from both sides of the building, and friendly staff who know how to mix a good Martini, clean or dirty. The nachos are particularly good too. It's not at all cluttered, with lots of space between tables and seating, making it good for an intimate drink too - a very good date spot.

Centre Point

...is my #1 London Landmark. Not because of any appreciation for the building's architecture, its tower block design not really being my style, but because as long as I can see it, I know how to get to Central London, and more specifically, Soho. This is helped by its blue top, a beacon for the lost.

There have been many occasions when I've been turned around in London and lost my bearings, not recognising any of the buildings or at least not knowing where to go upon seeing a partially familiar building. Every single one of those times, I've looked for the Centre Point tower, and when I successfully find it, it isn't long until I'm back on track and know which direction I'm heading in. Of course, I can't always see it from where I am, that's when I either walk in the direction I think the river is in (another great waypoint) or go to the nearest tube station if I can find it!

...bus stops are also a great tool for finding your way around the city, with just basic geographical knowledge. The fact that they now have 'Towards...' on them and most seem to have maps of the local area and slightly beyond is a huge help.

17 Pieces

For those asking why I simply don't just stop and ask for directions, no, it isn't because I'm too shy or embarrassed, if I was in desperate need, I wouldn't hesitate to ask, but I find it more fun to try and find my own way. Wandering aimlessly is one of the greatest things you can do in London - it's how I found most of my favourite places!

NBS, Bloomsbury

New Bloomsbury Set (NBS) is a lovely little off-scene, just-out-of-Soho basement bar in the heart of Bloomsbury. There are sofas, armchairs, tables & chairs, and two fantastic cave-like hangout areas, each with a TV where shows like The X Factor can and have been watched. The bar staff are lovely, quick to serve, and beautiful, and the owners are often themselves on-site, enjoying a drink with their patrons and ensuring everyone is having a good time! They also run several promotions, such as £10 for a bottle of House Wine at certain times, further reducing the already relatively cheap prices.

It's one of those places that can get busy, but isn't cramped or too loud, ideal for both post-work & pre-club drinks and get togethers. I've celebrated my Outiversary, friends' birthdays, and New Year's Eve here, all of which were the fun nights they should have been. It is one of those rare places that feels like it could be a local, somewhere you could go regularly, where the staff will know your name and your preferred drink, somewhere that you can become part of the already comfortable furniture.

The Black Cap, Camden

This is a rarity of a place, in that if you walked in off the street, you wouldn't at first realise that it is a gay bar. But it is, it really is. The upstairs bar is cosy and has the feel of a slightly camp local pub, with an excellent selection of bar food - very good sausages & mash!! Then out onto the covered terrace area with plenty of bench seating, perfect for summer evenings.

However, the greatest thing about The Black Cap, is the club downstairs. It's a bar with a dance floor and mini-stage, and what it lacks in size it makes up for in character and performances, most notably the Drag acts. If you've never seen a Drag act before, I suggest you see one at The Black Cap. I don't know if it's because of the smaller, more intimate surroundings, but all of those that I've seen here are phenomenal. It is easier here for them to call people up to the stage to be ridiculed, and mock the audience for their choice in clothing or drunken state...and bless the straight men who find themselves in their crosshairs!

Everyone basically gets on, no one takes themselves too seriously, and no one ever seems to take offence - if you're easily offended, you're probably best staying away from Drag acts all together. Beyond the Drag acts, the music selection is pretty fantastic, from cheesy pop to contemporary pop, dance hits and dance remixes. It is entirely unpretentious, where the only reason people look at you is to check you out, not once suggesting that you don't belong.

Hampstead Heath, Parliament Hill and the King William IV Pub

One of the most beautiful places in London with sweeping views, seemingly endless grassland, and clusters of trees, Hampstead Heath & Parliament Hill is always my first choice for a summer picnic or spot to watch the world go by from. I don't know if there's a higher more open green space in London, but it seems unlikely. It's difficult to put into words just how wonderful this place is, everything seems calmer, stiller on the Heath, and it never runs out of space - even at the height of summer, when much of London takes to the Heath to sunbathe, kick a ball about or throw a frisbee, or simply eat, drink and be very merry.

One of my favourite memories of the Heath & the King William IV pub - surely one of London's oldest gay pubs, is from my 29th birthday. Some of my friends and I had planned a picnic on the Heath, but it poured with rain, and I mean poured. So, we relocated to the King William IV pub on Hampstead High Street, one of my favourite London pubs - gay or otherwise, whose staff are some of the friendliest I've ever met, and whose food is bloody good! It is entirely unpretentious, everyone is welcome, and the locals and regulars all smile and give a friendly nod - it's one of those places where anyone could go and sit on their own, and not feel uncomfortable. It also has a lovely outside space, a favourite of mine for Saturday afternoons and drinks with friends.

We drank - I was already pretty tipsy when I got there (having been very, very drunk at a friend's wedding the night before!), we played games - birthday presents from friends, including drawing diagrams of my 'Network of Men' (as one friend so eloquently put it), we laughed, and I recovered from the night before.

Finally, the rain eased off, and some of us decided to head to the Heath for sunset. The five of us walked to the Heath, plonked ourselves down on my favourite bench on Parliament Hill and watched as London's sky changed from blue to grey to charcoal and finally to the darkness of late evening - or at least as dark as the London sky can get. It was one of those moments of no effort, everyone just doing it because it would be a nice thing to do, it's one of those moments that I go back to in my mind when my day isn't going well. Those moments are so important to make, save and remember.

Pentonville Road & Penton Rise

As you walk along Pentonville Road from Angel, passing the pubs and not really much else, that I noticed anyway, you can see various buildings on the horizon far out in front of you. But, as you get to Penton Rise, just above the top of the trees can be seen one of my favourite pieces of London architecture - St Pancras Railway Station, and more specifically the St Pancras Station Clock Tower.

As you walk, more and more of the tower and the building it is part of is revealed, until you eventually reach the end of Pentonville Road and the full beauty and true splendor of the tower and the main building is revealed. Thank you Sir John Betjeman for leading the charge against those who wanted to demolish it in the 60's!

Postman's Park & Christchurch Greyfriars Garden

Easily my favourite place within The City of London, Postman's Park is home to George Frederic Watt's 'Memorial to Heroic Self Sacrifice', one of the most beautiful and moving memorials I've ever seen. A wall of tablets with information about those who have sacrificed themselves to help others, with the newer memorial tablets designed to fit in with the originals of the 1900's. There are places to sit and think about those who have fallen and continue to fall in self sacrifice, be reminded of what is truly important in life, and ponder life's greater mysteries and questions.

Christchurch Greyfriars Garden is just a short walk from Postman's Park and offers a different type of experience. The garden of rose beds and hedges sits within the ruins and boundary of an old church which was heavily damaged during the Blitz. Wooden towers show where the original pillars would have stood, holding the church roof in place. It is one of those places that too few people seem to know about, but should, having been there for centuries in various forms and even managing to survive and outlive the Blitz - in one form or another. It is a shining example of how we can and should recycle areas that can't really be used for much else, and it is literally a place where you can take your time to smell the roses.

SOS, Charterhouse Street (Farringdon)

Smiths of Smithfield is my favourite place for brunch (followed closely by The Breakfast Club in Angel, then Giraffe at the Southbank Centre). There is something about the setup, the cleanliness, chrome surfaces, sofas, and the friendly, enthusiastic staff who are quick on their feet and have fantastic memories. It is an incredibly well-run operation, with a very varied menu - and gorgeous smoothies, which is why it is so popular at the weekend, so make sure you pre-book!

This has been the location of many a morning-after-the-night-before brunch, where the calm professionalism, quick service and Sunday papers on the sofas are one of the best cures you can ask for, followed closely by the fruity feel-good smoothies and my personal favourite, the best smoked salmon & scrambled eggs on toast ever. Ever. This is where I've celebrated friends' birthdays, again usually the morning-after-the-night-before, debated health and education policy with fellow Labourites over coffee and further gorgeous breakfast items (the 'Lumber Jack Stack' being another favourite), and lunchtime treats such as the fantastically done Cod Fish Finger Sandwich - I've tried a lot of these in a lot of places, this is one of the best!

It is well worth the trip to East Central London, especially with Postman's Park & Christchurch Greyfriars Garden just down the road.

LEON, Bankside/Soho/Spitalfields/Strand

...and probably all the others. 'LEON is me' is something a friend said about me a few years ago, and is also something that is on my Twitter profile. The reason? I share LEON's love of good, fresh, food. It is that simple. I have all of their cookbooks and have probably made about a third of the dishes from them, often times those being the dishes that people request for my next dinner party.

However, my love of LEON is more than just about the food, though that is a huge part of it - if you've tasted it, you'll understand why, if you haven't, you really should! It is about the people. Never have I come across such welcoming, happy, knowledgeable staff, as I do when I walk into any LEON restaurant. You can tell them what you're in the mood for, how hungry you are, and they will come up with a list of suggestions, and in an entirely non-pushy, non-sales way - which, if you're someone like me, is much more likely to get you more sales and future visits.

My first LEON experience was at LEON Bankside behind the Tate Modern, it is an open, aptly modern, welcoming place with easy to read food boards, far-too-tempting baked goods, LEON cook books, and fridges of fresh juices and the like. It was here that I first tasted Houmous, off a friend's plate, and it is that same Houmous & Flatbread that

I order as a starter every time I go to LEON. The difficult thing is choosing what main to have, never has there been a menu on which I have tasted and loved the majority of the dishes, which is why I rarely only order one.

My love for LEON became something else a couple of years ago, when I put myself forward to have my photo displayed on the 'Cook Book Library' wall in their then-new, now-closed (that was a truly sad day!) Soho branch. I went along to their Spitalfields branch, talked about my favourite cookbook which I'd brought with me (it was the cook book I learnt to bake from), had my photo taken with the book - and a pencil behind my ear, as you do, and within a couple of weeks, there I was framed and smiling on the wall, a copy of my beloved cook book behind me on the shelves of the 'Cook Book Library'.

So, if you are in Central London and you want excellent food with excellent service, there is one place to go: LEON (there are actually many places to go since LEON has multiple branches)

The Southbank Centre

Anyone and everyone can enjoy something about the Southbank Centre, from sitting alone reading a book or writing, to having a drink with friends, or seeing a performance, installation or exhibition. National Poetry Day Live & World Book Night are absolute musts for literature lovers, and they have a constantly changing, evolving programme of events covering what seems like every aspect of the arts. In summer, the terrace is bustling with people, but you can usually find somewhere to perch with your jug of PIMMS.

If you are visiting London for just a few days, make sure the

Southbank Centre is one of the places you check out, it is a real microcosm of London, and something that really shouldn't be missed.

Piccadilly

Piccadilly, like the Edgware Road, plays a central part in my life. It is in a road just off here that I would meet Zack for lunch or dinner & drinks after work. Green Park, both the station & the actual park have become central meeting points for various outings, and the park itself has been the site of many a picnic, wander and summertime afternoon of writing.

But, Piccadilly is on the list for something bigger. From home to Dollis Hill station, onto Green Park station, then down Piccadilly. It is the street that leads me to Soho. It is down this street that I have walked to see old friends and new, meet up with fellow Labour comrades for some campaigning, and see a new potential boyfriend for a first date.

The walk down Piccadilly can be quite the mission, full of lost tourists and sudden-stoppers - people who suddenly and without warning, stop in the middle of the pavement to take a picture or look at something. So, I've made it into a dance of sorts...weaving in between people, sometimes spinning or pivoting on one foot or heel, skimming sideways between groups of people, all in an entirely flawless example of graceful movement, obviously. Dancing down Piccadilly is how most of my Friday evenings begin.

17 Pieces

KU Bar, Lisle Street

KU Bar on Lisle Street, was the second Gay bar I'd been to when I first stepped through its doors in 2008, and it has played a pretty prominent role in my social and love life since. It was here that I first met Isaac after an LGBT Labour campaigning session, it was here that I was introduced to my now very good friend, George, and it was here that Zack told me we weren't going to be together anymore.

It is also the place where I drunkenly kissed an American, knowing nothing else about him except for the fact that he was a huge fan of U.S President Franklyn D. Roosevelt (as I am), where I also kissed a friend, told him he was coming home with me, then promptly (in a drunken stupor) forgot he was supposed to be coming with me and got on a tube home, alone - "Get your coat, I'm leaving" has been a punchline for quite a few years now! It has also been home to X Factor Saturdays & World AIDS Day fundraisers - where every year the staff and patrons do an amazing thing in raising money for excellent LGBT services.

So, it is incredibly difficult to sum up exactly what KU Bar means to me. In the simplest of terms, it is a place where things are always happening. It has been at the centre of some of my happiest and man-related times, a place where you can pop in for one or stay for the evening - before heading downstairs to KU Klub.

The Yard, Soho

This is my regular spot, it's rare for me not to be here at some point during a night out. Indeed, if I'm walking around Soho with friends trying to decide where to go, I will automatically, naturally, without thought, start walking towards The Yard. I can't think of a single night in The Yard that hasn't been happy or fun, and as is often the case with so many things that we like in life, I can't really put my finger on what makes it such a good bar. The staff are good, the drinks are well priced, the clientele is a real mix of Soho, mainly gay with the odd female work colleague or straight friend there for a party. It isn't at all pretentious. Perhaps it's a combination of all of those? The layout is probably a factor too, the Yard bar is accessed by a half-covered courtyard with tables and patio heaters, then upstairs in The Loft bar are sofas and tables with a balcony from which you can check out men as they enter the bar.

Of course, it may also be my favourite bar because it was the first gay bar I went in to after I came out to Ma. I entered alone, not knowing what to expect, but knowing that I had to face my fear and get over my nerves, so really, it is no wonder that it holds a special place in my heart. Throwing myself in at the deep end seems to have worked too.

Soho Square

One of the quieter, yet busier squares of Central London, Soho Square is a place where you can easily sit and people-watch for many hours. People strolling through, to and from work, colleagues on lunch breaks, students annotating and revising, the occasional Dishy Daddy or Yummy Mummy walking through with their children - likely called Oscar or Isabella, a writer or two sitting looking for inspiration in the faces of those that pass.

As beautifully serene as Soho Square can be, my favourite memories of it are when it is full of life, when we gays, lesbians, and all others of the LGBTQ+ community, accompanied by our straight friends, gather there during

17 Pieces

London Pride. The square comes alive with laughter and singing, the chatter of ever-excitable voices filling the air, almost as much as the scent of Gin & Tonic or White Wine in plastic cups, while breadstick crumbs line Houmous tubs and Chorizo-stained fingers search for wet wipes.

All the time, the sun (usually) shining through the trees like something from a Sundance Festival award winning Indie film. It is one the most beautiful days (and places) in London's Annual Calendar of Events.

Gone, but never forgotten:
Ghetto, between Charing Cross Road & Soho Square

Probably my favourite gay club of all time, perhaps joint first with Popstarz. Ghetto was nestled behind The Astoria, before it was torn down to make way for Crossrail... The reason for it being my favourite club is the reason why any good club night works, straight or gay: everyone was welcome.

On the part of the club, there was none of the gay:girl or guy:girl ratio counting that you get in some other clubs, and on the part of we, the clubbers, there was none of the judging, questioning, troublemaking nonsense you all too often hear about happening in other clubs. Everyone got on with it, everyone was there to have fun, dance until we couldn't dance any longer, drink very fairly priced drinks, and have a laugh with our friends. It was that simple. That, and the fact that never in my experience, before or since, has any other club had such a wide variety of gay men: cubs, twinks, jocks, geeks, otters, you name it, they had it. Then it was taken away.

I think Soho/Gay London is still yet to fill the unique hole left by Ghetto's Soho-based demise.

Dean Newby

AFTERWORD

Having completed the final pre-submission formatting of the book, I sat down, read through it, and then wrote this afterword. It covers three distinct areas; the book's common themes and events, lessons in writing for publication (as opposed to writing for fun/leisure), and my thoughts on the book as a whole.

Common themes and events

One of the interesting things to come out of collating the 17 pieces for this book, all of which were written separately over a two year period, was discovering that there are themes and ideas that many of the pieces share, beyond the obvious ones of love and memories - this is, after all a semi-autobiographical book about love.

There were three themes in particular that seemed to be fairly prominent across many of the pieces, they were:

i. the learning of lessons
ii. the often subtle and implicit nature of love
iii. the nature of what makes us the us we are

Dean Newby

In the first, the learning of lessons, I have for as long as I can remember, been aware of the importance of learning from experiences, of taking lessons from both the mistakes that you've made and the situations where you've been successful and achieved what you either wanted or needed.

The pieces of this book show that sometimes the lessons can seem tiny, insignificant even, but they aren't, no lesson is every truly insignificant because, something else I talk about a lot across the pieces, it is the sum of those experiences, how we felt and feel about them, and the lessons learnt from them that (can) have an impact on how we feel, act and react (essentially, how we behave) when faced with similar experiences and events in the future.

In the second, the often subtle and implicit nature of love, I, until fairly recently, wanted the love of grand gestures and explicit (not in the sex sense) outspoken romance, the type of love you see on TV programmes and films - you've only got to look at some of my 'Music Seen' scenes to see that! But, Isaac started to change that - the kitchen hug and the potted sunflower, for example, and Zack really changed that, probably in part because of our pre-existing friendship and therefore ease to communicate such things in different ways, ways in which he knew I would understand - again, in the kitchen (kitchens seem to play a big part in my life) with that kiss, for instance.

After Zack, I really noticed and paid much more attention to the subtler ways in which people show love, the hand on the back of the head, the reassuring wink, even something as simple and seemingly mundane as making you a cup of tea when you're having/have had a hard day. Too many of those little things, those subtle, implicit acts, are overlooked in today's busy, demanding, uber-expectations world. We really do, all of us, need to take a little time to think about and be thankful for what we have in this world, or rather, who we have.

In the third, the nature of what makes us the us we are, I came to realise just how much I believe the impact of others has on us as individuals, and how much the things we do and experience can impact the us we eventually become - as well as the idea that that very same 'us' is a never ending evolution, our personalities changing and adapting to our environments, while the core of our being, our key, primary personality traits remain the same, guiding us along that path of personality development.

I also realised that to me, personality is definitely much more than a set of traits. It is those traits, and those events and feelings we experience throughout life, but it is also the decisions we make and the paths we take, the philosophies and principles we develop along the way, and the friends (and foes) we meet whose influence has a direct, and sometimes indirect impact on those philosophies and principles.

We are the sum of our life's experiences, the greater the contrast of those experiences, the more we (can) grow as a person. Always questioning, always learning, always growing.

There were also two events that seemed to quite clearly have an impact on me, since they are both mentioned more than once and across various pieces - some of which are not about or centered around those events. These were:

i. my mum and dad's breakup
ii. my grandad's death

While it was of no surprise that both of these were discussed, I was surprised by how much they were either discussed, referenced, or had some sort of off-page impact on what I was remembering and therefore writing.

My mum and dad's breakup had a profound impact on me, but not, as previously discussed in 'In Safe Hands', in the way in which you might expect. It was, for all intents and purposes, a turning point. A new path had opened up, one with different boundaries and expectations, one which would allow my relationship with Ma to be more than the traditional one of mother and son, but of friendship. One relationship began to fade, while another became something more than it had been before that point, that relationship of course being the one with my grandad.

Before my grandad's death I'd never seen anyone die before, and had no idea that it would be, in fact even that it could be, a comforting thing. That sounds odd, I know, obviously I was upset, in fact I was numb until my cousins arrived at the hospital (where I was smoking cigarette after cigarette in the cold January night, idiot), and I started thinking about our unborn children never meeting him and all of the sorts of things we think about when someone we're close to dies.

But, having seen my grandad in his last moments of life, knowing that he hadn't been in any pain, that he was peaceful and simply seemed to drift off to sleep was a real comfort. Beyond that initial sense of comfort, and in fact the loss of a grandparent, I had lost a friend, one of my oldest friends, a friend with whom so many good times had been shared, with whom so much of my life was intertwined. I cannot overemphasise our friendship and the impact he and it had and still has on my life, and so it really is no surprise that his death was yet another turning point in my life.

I had already been living my life using the lessons he had taught, and those I had picked up from others along the way, but, after his death, I really embraced them, in fact it was this embracing that would lead to my leaving my job at the local college to set up my own business.

The lessons from my grandad and others, and those I have thought of myself, are written in a notebook that I almost always have with me...perhaps one day, I'll publish them and their stories too.

Lessons in writing for publication

There are two distinct things I've learnt about writing something that you intend to publish...

1. it can be as easy or as difficult as you want it to be.

2. you have to be strict with your deadlines, but not to the detriment of your book.

Neither of these even enter my thinking when I'm writing for pleasure/at my leisure, it is always easy - otherwise I couldn't consider it pleasurable, and there are no deadlines, so you can write as much or as little whenever you like. Writing for publication, well, that's a different story...but, it is one that can still be an enjoyable experience, as long as you don't get too stressed (with yourself) about the writing, formatting, and everything else that comes with publishing - and where self-publishing is involved, it seems there is a lot more to do, especially if you want to do it well and make it the best it can be!

There is one distinct thing I've learnt about myself both as a writer and in general, and that is that I am an absolute perfectionist. I've always known that, indeed Ma Newby remembers me screwing up entire pages of work because I'd made one mistake (high maintenance much?!), but in my writing and collating of 17 Pieces, I discovered that so strong is my desire for perfection, that at times when my writing was anything but or the book as a whole wasn't flowing as I'd envisaged it, I hit a creative wall.

I was only able to overcome that creative block by walking away from that particular piece or scenario, and coming back to it later on. Every time, without fail, I was able to get back in to either the writing or formatting, tweaking bits here and there, changing vocabulary, until finally it was as I wanted it...and some weeks over my self-imposed deadline. But, I would rather be happy with it and a little behind schedule, than unhappy or consider it 'satisfactory' to be on schedule - especially since it is a self-set deadline.

I've no doubt that my usual need for perfection was heightened because this is to be my first published work, and more than that, is autobiographical in nature, and as such should be, must be, an absolute work of sheer perfection, but I have learnt a very valuable lesson in (self) expectation and deadline setting!

Thoughts on the book as a whole

To me, this book is everything I had hoped and wanted it to be, and while I have my own favourite pieces, there isn't a single one that I don't like. I hope you feel the same, or at the very least, have one or two pieces that you like or have been able to relate to?

In writing about the types of love I'd experienced and the impact they'd had on me, I inadvertently discovered what my idea of love really is, and was able to define what attributes, characteristics and emotions were important to me in any loving relationship. It's really quite simple when you think about it:

> Respect, Honesty, Kindness, and Loyalty
> *(and the 'Indefinable')*

Those are the core four (exc. the indefinable, since it is by its very nature, indefinable), of course there are many other attributes to choose from, but those are the four without which I don't believe a truly loving, healthy relationship, be that with a lover, friend, or family member, can exist. Those are my four, you probably have your own, love is, after all, a deeply personal and individual thing. I think 17 Pieces and the fact that there are 17 pieces, shows that.

Dean Newby

THE KICKSTARTER PROJECT

As I mentioned in the Acknowledgements section, this book would not have been possible had it not been for the generosity shown by so many through their pledging to and backing of the 17 Pieces Kickstarter Project.

For those of you who don't know what Kickstarter is, it is a crowdfunding platform that allows ordinary people like me to seek funding for a project from other people. The funding is based on pledgers wanting to see a project that they are interested in come to fruition, and be a part of that process in some way.

Kickstarter offered me the opportunity to communicate with my potential pledgers and readers, to involve them in the process of writing, and particularly collating my book. Through regular updates and the integral 'Any Pledge, 3 Votes' pledging reward - which meant that anyone who pledged had 3 votes that could be used to vote for the pieces they wanted included in the final book - 5 pieces were 'Core Pieces' and were already included in the book, meaning that the voters would choose the remaining 12 pieces. I was certain that I could get people interested in the book. It worked.

Pledges soon began coming in, at first from family and friends, then from their friends (social networks in action!), and then one of the really exciting moments happened...

A stranger, someone I didn't know, someone my family and friends didn't know, pledged to the project.
To think that someone was willing to put up money for a project by someone they didn't know, to put not just faith in me and the project, but financial assistance, was one of the most moving moments of the project - that, and the moment that we crossed the funding line with 3 weeks to spare (at which point I did a little spontaneous dance around my room)

That is the brilliance of Kickstarter, the ease with which prospective pledgers can find a project to back. Part of that brilliance is the Kickstarter Community, those who use Kickstarter and pledge, and in wanting a project to be a success, use the greatest marketing technique of all time, 'word-of-mouth', to encourage other people to pledge and be a part of bringing someone's project to fruition.
Soon enough, the project was across the funding line (if you don't get 100% of funding, you don't get a penny), and we were at 110%, then 120, 130, eventually finishing at 144% funding!! So many people had pledged to the project and backed my dream of publishing my book, a book that had been two years in the making, that started as a letter to an ex, and even when I was guaranteed the money for the project (having reached 100%), the pledges were still rolling in - people were showing that it wasn't just about getting me to the finish line, it was about them wanting to be a part of it, of wanting to support me and my dream.

17 Pieces

Some brief project numbers:

- 21% of pledgers found the project using Kickstarter, with the remaining 79% being directed there from various social networks and internet searches.

- there were 68 pledgers in total

- the average pledge was £20.74

- 21 pledgers pledged at the £7 pledging level (which included an eBook copy), while 16 pledged at the £17 pledging level (which included an eBook copy and a paperback copy)

- the project video was watched 113 times

- 10 Updates to pledgers & prospective pledgers were posted before the project ended

- 1 Dean Newby was gobsmacked, speechless even, which for me is very rare.

With the project successful end, it was time for the pledgers to start voting. I divided the pieces into 3 sections, to ensure that the final book would have varied content, and created a further 2 sections which contained all of the pieces. Voters could use 1 vote per section, and in Sections 4 & 5 had free votes, meaning they could vote for a piece they had already voted for, should they wish to do so.

The Result (this is the update that was sent to all pledgers)

After much spreadsheet geekery, which was probably more fun than it should have been, we have the results of the 17 Pieces Selection Vote!!

Dean Newby

In total, 38 (55.9%) eligible voters placed their votes. All 'voting papers' were completed, with one vote placed in each section.

The results were calculated in the following way:

Pieces 1-10: The two pieces with the most votes from each of the 5 sections
Pieces 11 & 12: The two pieces with the most combined free votes (Section 4 + Section 5)
This was to strike a balance between the themes (as per sections 1-3) and what the voters really wanted to read regardless of their section (the free vote, sections 4 & 5)

As such, in order of highest to lowest, with: section & number of votes indicated in brackets:

Pieces 1-10:
The Girls are back in Town (Section: 1 - Votes: 11)
Defenders of the Faith (Section: 2 - Votes: 10)
Unrequited U (Section: 3 - Votes: 10)
Love...?! (Section: 2 - Votes: 9)
Chain Reaction (Section: 1 - Votes: 8)
Music Seen (Section: 3 - Votes: 8)
Equals with a side of Pork (Section: 4 - Votes: 7)
Lost Love, Lost Us (Section: 4 - Votes: 5)
In Safe Hands (Section: 5 - Votes: 4)
Hair Today (Section: 5 - Votes: 4)

Pieces 11 & 12:
LondonFound (6)
The Italian Stallion (5)

Other bits of voting related trivia:
From the outset, both 'The Girls are back in Town' & 'Unrequited U' were the two favourites.

At least 2 pieces that each person voted for will be included in the book.

7 people will get to read all 5 of the pieces they voted for, as they cast all of their votes for pieces that will be included in the book - the maximum anyone could vote for.

Every vote, bar 1, cast for 'The Girls are back in Town' was cast by a woman, with it also being the piece that women placed the most votes for.

The higher ranges of male votes were evenly split between 4 or 5 pieces, with no one piece being more popular.

'Unrequited U' was particularly popular among voters in the 'Friend' category, while 'The Girls are back in Town' was most popular among voters in the 'Work-related Friends' category.

So, I finally had my 17 pieces and work began on editing, with a few minor rewrites along the way - and, as I said in the Afterword, a whole lot of perfectionism.

The next step is to get people buying my book, this book...for that, I will once again be enlisting the help of friends and family, and everyone else who pledged to the Kickstarter Project!!

Dean Newby

REFERENCES

Music:

Basshunter. "Angel in the Night." [Single] Hard2Beat Records, 2008. CD Single.

Bon Iver. "Flume." *For Emma, Forever Ago.* 4AD, 2008. CD.

Gabrielle. "Give Me A Little More Time." *Gabrielle.* Go! Beat, 1996. CD. (Gabrielle, Barson, Wolff, Dean)

Jenkins, Karl. "Tintinnabulum." *Songs of Sanctuary.* Venture, 1995. CD.

Kool & The Gang. "Celebration." *Celebrate!* Mercury, 1980. Vinyl LP.

McCartney, Paul. "We All Stand Together." [Single] Parlophone, 1984. Vinyl Single.

Mumford & Sons. "Lover of the Light" *Babel.* Island Records, 2012. CD.

Nilsson, Harry. "Without You." *Nilsson Schmilsson.* RCA Victor, 1971. CD. (Evans & Ham)

17 Pieces

Reeves, Jim. "Silver Bells." *12 Songs of Christmas*. RCA Camden, 1963. Vinyl LP.
(Evans & Livingston)

Sparro, Sam. "I Wish I Never Met You." *Return to Paradise*. EMI, 2012. CD.
(Sparro, Rogg, Hassle)

St. John, Peter. (writer) "The Fields of Athenry." c.1970
[Irish Folk Song]

Film:

The Adventures of Robin Hood. Michael Curtiz & William Keighley. Warner Bros, 1938. Film.

Television:

The X-Files. Sky. 1997. Television.

ABOUT THE AUTHOR

I was born to a mother who loves to write poetry and read whatever she can get her hands on, and a father who would leave her limericks on the coffee table. Add to that an extended family of avid readers, an uncle who could enthuse you about writing within minutes of simply talking about it, some brilliant English teachers, and the friends made along the way, and you have me.

It seems that I have always written, from short stories as a child, to poetry as a teen, always writing. Writing is my main form of relaxation, where I can enter a world of my memories or imaginings, something that feels very natural and unforced.

In 2004, I started my own business, one of the benefits of which being the extra time I would have to write, and so, I did.

9 years later...here I am, finally publishing a piece of work!"

I'd love to hear your thoughts on the book, love, anything 17 Pieces related, so please do get in touch on either: Twitter (@dean_newby -or- @17Pieces), Facebook (Page: 17 Pieces), or via e-mail: reader@17pieces.co.uk

Thanks for reading!
Dean Newby

Printed in Great Britain
by Amazon